POLAND, 1919-1945

POLAND

AND

RUSSIA

1919-1945

JAMES T. SHOTWELL

Bryce Professor, Emeritus, History of International Relations,
Columbia University. Director, Division of Economics and History,
Carnegie Endowment for International Peace.

MAX M. LASERSON

Visiting Professor of Philosophy, Columbia University.
Formerly Professor at the Riga Graduate School of Economics, and
Assistant Professor of Constitutional Law, St. Petersburg University.

Published for THE CARNEGIE ENDOWMENT FOR
INTERNATIONAL PEACE
By KING'S CROWN PRESS, New York

1945

KING'S CROWN PRESS

is a division of Columbia University Press organized for the purpose of making
certain scholarly material available at minimum cost. Toward that end, the
publishers have adopted every reasonable economy except such as would interfere
with a legible format. The work is presented substantially as submitted by the
author, without the usual editorial attention of Columbia University Press.

Foreword

THIS STUDY is one of a number planned, by the Division of Economics and History of the Carnegie Endowment for International Peace, to deal with the postwar settlement and the political problems of Europe. Among these questions, that of the western frontiers of the U.S.S.R. is of fundamental importance, as the years 1919 to 1939 have clearly shown. The frontier controversy which came up for settlement at the Paris Peace Conference in 1919 dealt with more than a shifting of territorial sovereignty. In reality "the Curzon Line" is the outer symbol of inner movements within the Slavic peoples of central and eastern Europe and the settlement of such sovereignty is more than a mere geographic determination of boundaries.

Out of the ruins of the old Austro-Hungarian and Russian Empires, which had crumbled during the first World War, and out of defeated Germany, were formed new or enlarged or restored Slav states impinging more closely than ever before upon the Germanic population of central Europe. This increased Slavic pressure in central Europe was, in the eyes of Nazi Germany, a sufficient excuse for a second World War to end all danger from Slavdom, by the complete overthrow of Soviet Russia. The preparation of German National Socialism for this crusade began almost immediately after the conclusion of the Treaty of Versailles. Nowhere is the duty of the German to overthrow the Slav more strongly stated than in *Mein Kampf*. This war aim of Hitler was stated in its crudest form in the Führer's speech at the Nuremburg Party Day celebration of 1936, in which he reminded his followers of the "incalculable wealth of raw materials" which lay beyond the Urals and of the "unending cornfields of the Ukraine," pointing out that if these "lay within Germany under the National Socialist leadership, the country would swim in plenty."

When one recalls that Teutonic antagonism to the Slav is centuries old, then one can realize the extremely difficult position of a frontier Slav state like Poland. This phase of the question is, however, one which involves so many other considerations of high politics that they cannot be dealt with in this short study, limited as it is to the relations between Soviet Russia and Poland.

It should be added that the study does not make recommendations but is an analysis of the attitudes of the parties to the dispute and of those interested in its settlement.

The authors wish to express their sincere appreciation of the editorial assistance rendered by Miss Marina Salvin and of the technical skill and tireless effort of Mrs. Rose Klima, in the preparation of this volume under difficult conditions.

JAMES T. SHOTWELL
MAX M. LASERSON

Contents

Introduction

THIS VOLUME deals with a subject in which, as the history is being written, it is also being made. But while the narrative is necessarily incomplete, the guiding principles which determine policies have already become clear. The "Polish question" is a political question, and political questions are less concerned with the substance of the dispute than with the attitudes of the disputants toward each other. No one, not even the most highly qualified geographer, could trace a perfect boundary among the various peoples on Poland's eastern frontier. Along most of the way an equally good argument could be made for a line some miles, or some score of miles, east or west of that chosen. The inhabitants of the villages in the Pripet Marshes care less, from all accounts, about the rival Polish and Russian claims than the politicians who are vocal on their behalf. The heart of the difficulty for re-establishing peaceful relations in eastern Europe is that neighboring nations do not trust each other. This is the heritage of centuries of war and oppression. It cannot be eradicated over night. But the ultimate settlement of the Polish question will have to be found in the elimination of hate and fear, and that can only happen by the imposition of a lasting peace which will outlaw the resort to violence.

It must be at once admitted that this generalization will seem to some like putting the cart before the horse; that we must have a *just* territorial settlement in eastern Europe before we can think of eliminating the threat of war from politics. While this is fundamentally true, it still leaves open the question as to who shall decide what is just. When nationalism runs riot what seems justice to one nation often seems the height of injustice to its neighbor, and in an atmosphere of fear and hatred the motives for any political action are likely to be denounced as hostile and an incitation to conflict. But security can no longer be sought in power politics. That is the fundamental lesson of two World Wars.

It must be kept in mind that the tracing of frontiers is only partly determined by the local situation on the frontier itself. There is also the question of national security—the effort to obtain a good defensive line against a possible invasion. This war has shown, however, that no boundary, however well defended, even by a Siegfried Line, is a sure guardian of a nation's territory. Its security lies in its political strength among other nations. This used to be sought in combinations of power politics, but two World Wars have shown us that there is no more safety in such alliances than in reliance upon the natural geographic defences of the country. The only safety for a country like Poland lies in the support which it can count upon when in danger of attack, and that, in turn, depends upon the erection of a better international system than that of a balance of power. If Poland has to depend upon either Russia or Germany, in the future, or upon balancing one off against the other, there would merely be a recrudescence of ancient hatreds resulting in an ultimate resort to force in which Poland would again be a victim along with one or both of its great neighbors.

The Polish question therefore is to a large extent the first great test of the plans of the United Nations to make good their adherence to the fundamental principles adopted at San Francisco.

This study is to some extent a basic document for dealing with that phase of the Polish question which is most in evidence today. It therefore deals primarily, but not wholly, with a territorial question. But any student of history knows that territorial questions which are serious enough to stir the fires of international discord are not so much questions of geography as of history. No people have been more conscious of their history than the Poles, perhaps in compensation for the fact that they have been deprived of it in recent times. On the other hand, Soviet Russia is only now becoming history-conscious. The Bolshevist revolutionaries who surrendered this disputed territory in the revolutionary years have now acquired a wholly different attitude. Partly as a result of the war, and partly because of a maturing political organization, the country of the Soviets has developed a sense of nationalism which links it with the Russia of the past. The result is that the unyielding temper of the Soviet Government with reference to its claims on its European frontier is shared to the full by all Russians everywhere, including refugees from Bolshevism in other lands. This unity of purpose is so strong that it is doubtful if any Russian government, even a democratic one, would under the circumstances fail to claim the territory up to the Curzon Line, thus recovering the land lost in the Polish-Soviet war and ceded to Poland in the treaty of Riga, in 1921. Such unity unquestionably is a strong factor underlying the declaration of war against Japan. This statement undoubtedly holds with reference to the Baltic States and other frontiers of the U.S.S.R. The new Russian nationalism is a political fact of the first magnitude. It is partly a result of the war, but also partly of the systematic development of the Soviet State.

But nowhere else has nationalism played a stronger role than in Poland; and nowhere else has there been such a violation of a nation's territories.

That Polish nationalism was able to survive, and Polish culture maintain its proud record of achievement, is one of the miracles of the history of Europe. The great powers, far from destroying it, have hammered it white upon the anvil of imperialism until it has become an instrument of international policy. But it is an instrument which cannot be used as effectively for the settlement of Poland's boundary questions as some of the champions of Poland's case seem to think. For when nationalism clashes against nationalism, the settlement is determined by power. It is therefore of the utmost importance for Poland that the advocacy of Poland's claims should rest upon another basis than that of the age-old use of force, or diplomacy based on force. The only lasting settlement satisfactory to Poland and its neighbors is one which must correspond to the real needs of the people most concerned, who are the inhabitants of the territories in question.

To recognize that a just settlement offers the best advantages to all concerned is not altruism but *Realpolitik,* a German word which must be translated into a more civilized meaning if we are to have peace in the world. If the Polish question is ever to be settled, and there is no reason why it should not be, we must look behind diplomatic and military history based on territorial sovereignty; for that does not reach to the heart of the problem. Behind the territorial struggle there lies another. The question of the frontier line has been but the symbol of a cleavage between the governments of Poland and Russia, for Poland's mighty neighbor on the east holds to a social and economic philosophy which has been repugnant to many Poles, and particularly to those loyal to the Government-in-Exile.

It is this fundamental fact which has made a difficult compromise seem insoluble. In the controversy, the initial advantage has lain with the U.S.S.R., not only because of its greater power, but also because it still speaks, although with less militant accent, in the language of revolution. As it grapples with the problems of the present and future, it is therefore relatively unhampered by the past. Although its new nationalism is steadily sinking its roots in history, it never loses sight of the fact that there are vital forces which determine the course of events fully as much as, if not more than, any diplomatic arrangements between governments. The greatest of these forces is economics. In the present case, this means the use of the land. It is short-sighted and misleading for us to think of the wide stretching plain on the west of Russia and the east of Poland in terms only of political sovereignty over them. For those who cultivate these fields and whose homes are in the hamlets on the countryside, the land is for the purpose of raising food and maintaining life, a fact daily driven home in the hard struggle with nature. Throughout the centuries this peasantry has looked upon the fields and woodlands less in terms of political allegiance than of a homeland beyond whose borders they had little interest. This, as we shall see in the course of this study, is especially true of the White Russians.

Therefore we should not be surprised to find that the problem of agrarian reform is now emerging as of major importance in the settlement. If, for example, Soviet Russia can speedily restore prosperity to its ravaged lands as well as to its cities, it will have a stronger influence over its neighbors than by any increase of military force. On the other hand, the attitude of the Polish Government-in-Exile toward land reform has been a source of weakness and is one of the main elements in the division between the Polish leaders themselves.

The Warsaw Provisional Government, whose members now form the majority in the Provisional Government of National Unity, has held that the settlement of the Polish question is possible only on the basis of a full acceptance of the agrarian land reform decree discussed below, and of the substitution of the more democratic Constitution of 1921 for that of 1935. This latter condition has been equally difficult for the London Poles to accept because it is under the 1935 Constitution that they hold power. Equally difficult would be the acceptance of land reform, because some of them are great land owners in the very area in question.

There is therefore a real division among the Poles themselves, and this was accentuated rather than lessened as the war progressed. The territorial settlement, however, has been taken out of the hands of both parties by the decision of the Yalta Conference in which both Great Britain and the United States substantially agreed to the Russian claims. The Conference still left the door partly open for further negotiation. "The eastern frontier of Poland should follow the Curzon Line, with digressions from it in some regions of five to eight kilometers in favor of Poland." The opposition to this settlement by the Polish Government in London henceforth had only one practical political justification, that of securing adequate compensation for ultimately yielding to the inevitable.

The compensation suggested at Yalta, that Poland should receive "substantial accessions of territory in the north and west," was not well received by the Polish Government; for it would create lasting animosity on the part of Germany, and therefore make Poland more dependent upon Russia for its future security than would be consonant with the promises made to it in the past. As, however, this matter of the western frontier of Poland is left for "a final delimitation" at "the peace conference" to be held at the end of the war, it is impossible to pursue this suggestion further at the present time. There will be much diplomacy before it is settled.

1. The Curzon Line

ANY STUDY of the question of the eastern frontier of Poland should begin by defining it, first, with reference to the Polish problem as a whole, and second, with reference to the post-war settlements of Soviet Russia and the other United Nations. The territorial question of the so-called "Curzon Line" has been treated in some recent discussions as though it were the fundamental problem in the re-establishment and reconstruction of Poland. This perspective is wrong. It is true that the complex question of territory-cutting and territory-compensation will, when it is all decided upon, result in the creation of a new Poland different from any in past history; and that the shifting of frontiers will condition to some extent the economic life of the Polish people. Nevertheless, the fact will always remain that Poland is more than its frontiers—a fundamental fact, which should not be lost sight of in the midst of the discussion of the Curzon Line.

Similarly, the success or failure of the negotiations concerning the Curzon Line, while furnishing a test case for the United Nations, should not be allowed to interfere with the future capacity of the "General International Organization" of the Moscow Declaration in the application of the principles of the Atlantic Charter to other parts of the post-war settlements. A series of such questions is bound to develop now that Germany has been defeated and the vast areas occupied by her armies have been freed. When a country is made up of several different races, each with its own national consciousness, its restoration to a pre-war status becomes even more complicated. Difficulties, therefore, have appeared not only in Poland but also in other "multi-national" states like Yugoslavia, Czechoslovakia, Hungary and Rumania. For these, as for Poland, it is to be hoped that the harsh procedure of transferring entire ethnical groups by compulsion will not become a general technique for avoiding nationalist clashes in the future.

For Poland, the complexity of the problem is due to the circumstances of her history. When the Paris Peace Conference attempted, in 1919, to restore Poland to the map of Europe, that country had had no political existence for almost 125 years. The old Polish Kingdom which broke up in 1795 when it was partitioned among Russia, Prussia and Austria, had been a basically feudal country, but one which proudly cherished and desperately fought for its freedom and independence. It was doubly tragic for Poland that its national state ceased to exist almost at the very time the French Revolution began to spread the gospel of national statehood over Europe. Although there were Polish statesmen of that time who formulated the ideal of a progressive constitution, it was already too late. The three monarchies which divided the rich spoil of Poland were themselves based upon the ancient regime of feudal privilege and the result was to leave the then existing social order of Poland almost intact. The Polish nobles were, to be sure, deprived of their own royal court and their own state symbolism, but not of their feudal estates nor of their serfs, whether the latter were genuine Poles or Ukrainians and White Russians.

During the century that followed, the new and triumphant concept of the national state made such headway throughout Europe that when Poland was restored in 1919 it was not possible to revive the political and social conditions which prevailed a century and a quarter earlier. In the interval between 1795 and 1919, movements of a social, political and cultural character had developed among the Ukrainians and White Russians which began to stimulate national consciousness in these two border peoples. In the second half of the nineteenth century, Ukrainian East Galicia became for the oppressed Ukrainian minority of Czarist Russia a center of rebirth such as Piedmont had been for the Italians. The more these two Slavic peoples developed from their "unhistoric status" into political maturity, and even into a provisional independence, the less likely it became that they could ever be simply merged into a national community dominatd by the Poles.

These circumstances, together with Russia's absence from the discussions of the Paris Peace Conference, made it almost inevitable that, although Poland was restored as a state, its eastern frontiers should be left unsettled when the Versailles Treaty was signed on June 28, 1919. It was only on December 8, that in order to obviate the inconvenience of such a situation, the Supreme Council of the Allied and Associated Powers made a declaration establishing provisional eastern frontiers for Poland.[1] The provisional frontiers coincided approximately with the line later called the Curzon Line. The declaration concluded: "The rights which Poland could possibly have to territories situated east of the above-mentioned line are expressly reserved." It was signed by Clemenceau, but in the preparatory work and in the decisions a very active part was taken by the representatives of the United States, particularly by Dr. Robert H. Lord,[2] the specialist on Polish

1. "Without prejudging the provisions which must in the future define the Eastern frontiers of Poland, . . ." British State Papers, Volume 112, pp. 971-972 (French Text), London, 1922.

2. On March 18, 1945 Dr. Lord objected strongly to the present treatment of Poland by Russia and suggested a Russian-Polish frontier slightly east of the Curzon Line which

history on the American delegation to negotiate peace in 1919, and Mr. Frank L. Polk, former Under-Secretary of State.

The Curzon Line was an effort to establish a frontier on ethnographical rather than political lines in a part of the world where no satisfactory political frontier existed. In the north, along the Pripet River and Pripet marshes, the majority of the population is White Russian or White Ruthenian; in the south, it is Ukrainian. Ethnographically speaking, the northern section is merely a westward geographical continuation of that part of eastern White Russia which formerly belonged to the Soviet Union, under the name of the White Russian (Byelorusskaya) Soviet Socialist Republic. Likewise, the southern, or Ukrainian part of Eastern Poland is but a westward continuation of the eastern Ukraine or the Ukrainian Soviet Socialist Republic. The demographic gravity center of White Russia lies in the pre-war Soviet area. The whole population of White Russia has been estimated at about 10,000,000 inhabitants, while there were only about 1,500,000 White Russians in eastern pre-war Poland. As to the Ukrainians, the Soviet Ukrainians numbered roughly 30,000,000, while those in Poland were only about 6,000,000.[3] In the past, however, ethnographic statistics in that part of the world have never been accurate, although the nineteenth century statistics of the Austro-Hungarian portion of Poland are more reliable than those of Imperial Russia. The majority of the people, living on the soil and having little contact with the world outside, did not have the strong nationalist feeling of the peoples of western Europe. It is therefore misleading to adduce the statistical data of the past as though it were comparable to the statistics of the present. The Supreme Council of 1919 and its respective Commissions had, therefore, an almost impossible task in attempting to draw the eastern frontier of Poland. There is no question that the line ultimately proposed under the presidency of President Botha, afterward called the Curzon Line, was an honest effort to establish an ethnographic frontier between that part of Poland which has a decisive Polish majority and those parts later called Eastern Poland in which the White Russians and Ukrainians form a majority.

The population statistics for the disputed areas are not only basically difficult to arrive at in terms of past history but have been further falsified by the impact of the second World War. No one yet has any idea of the extent of the depopulation, extermination, and shifting of populations in that part of the world as a result of the German invasion and withdrawal.

would give to Poland the cities Vilna and Lwow. The compensation offered Poland in Pomerania, Silesia and Brandenburg is dangerous because it would create eternal enmity between Germany and Poland. "The Poles fear," says Dr. Lord, "the Russians might later offer to assure the return of these provinces to Germany as a bait by which to draw Germany into her orbit." *New York Times,* March 19, 1945.

3. See *Soviet Russia in Maps,* G. Goodall, Ed., London, 1942.

In general, however, it may be stated that the population of autonomous eastern Galicia, the territory delimited by the Supreme Council in 1919, was approximately a third Polish and more than half, or 51 per cent, Ukrainian, while the territory between the Curzon Line and the frontier established by the Riga Treaty, in 1921, outside of eastern Galicia contained about as many Poles as there were Ukrainians and White Ruthenians together.[4] The city of Lwow has always had a definite Polish majority of about 60 per cent. From the fourteenth century Lwow, remaining a well-populated Polish area in a Ukrainian environment, became, together with Warsaw, Poznan, and Cracow, one of the most important centers of Polish culture, particularly in the years of Austrian domination. Lwow had the well-known Ossolyneum museum and library where Polish scholars and publicists worked as research men, historians and bearers of Polish self-determination against the pressure of the three powerful monarchies.

When we turn from statistics to history, we are on relatively firmer ground, although the entire area of the Polish eastern frontier was at various times subjected to the changing influences of Polish, White Russian, Ukrainian and Russian dominance. The history of Polish-Russian relations shifted back and forth for almost a thousand years, registering the influence of the two great branches of the Christian Church, the Orthodox and the Catholic. The White Russians played the least important rôle in the development of this area, because the Ukrainians and Russians had the advantage of a long history of political independence and of struggles against invasion by the Mongols, the Tartars, the Turks, and other enemies. Nevertheless, from the establishment of the Polish-Lithuanian federation, in 1385, until the sixteenth century, White Russian was the official language of Lithuanian laws and politics, and the language of the White Russian gentry was adopted by the Lithuanians as best suited for state requirements. But as the upper classes became assimilated into a Polish environment, they were Polonized, while their peasantry was reduced to the level of serfs, leaving the village as the only center of spoken White Russian and of the continuation of traditional folklore and folkways. Thus the

4. Paprocki, in his book *Minority Affairs in Poland* (Warsaw, 1935), estimated the total number of the Ukrainians in Poland to be 4,870,000. They constituted, in the Voivodship of Stanislav, about three quarters of the general population and slightly less in the Voivodship of Volyn; about one-half in the Voivodship of Tarnopol, and about a third in the Voivodship of Lwow.

The total number of White Russians in Poland was 1,500,000. About half of these lived in a closed ethnic area, mostly in the Voivodship of Vilna, or the counties of Disna, Oshmiana, Braslav and Vileika; in the Voivodship of Novogrodek and the counties of Baranowicze, Slonim, and Nesviezh. There was also a White Russian enclave in the Voivodship of Bialystok with a majority in six counties. In all these areas together the White Russians made up three fourths of the population. But Paprocki himself expressed some doubt about the exactitude of his figures for the number of White Russians in Poland. (See pages 100-101.)

White Russians sank to the level of peoples without a national history of their own and remained on this level almost to the end of the nineteenth century.

A far greater rôle was played by the Ukrainians. They had formed an independent and primitively democratic state to the south and east of Russia and Poland. The first stage of Russian history centered around Kiev. For centuries the Ukraine, being predominantly a military state, participated in the defense of Poland and Russia against the Tartar hordes, the Crimean Tartars, the Turks, and various nomadic tribes of the steppes. It was on the basis of a free decision, though not without a certain amount of Ukrainian opposition, that the Ukraine was united to Russia in 1654, receiving in return guarantees of certain privileges and of the right of self-administration. But slowly the Ukrainians and their military aristocracy became merged with the Russian aristocracy and bureaucracy. Beginning, too, with the reign of Catherine II, the original privileges guaranteed to the Ukraine at the time of its merging with Russia diminished with ever-increasing rapidity. Under Czarist rule the masses of Ukrainian peasantry were reduced to serfdom, and the educated classes became either Polonized or Russianized. The Russian imperial ukase of 1867 prohibited even the printing of Ukrainian books and periodicals.

Basic changes came, however, after the abolition of serfdom and the beginning of the industrialization of the Ukraine and White Russia, with a consequent improvement in the social conditions of both the White Russians and the Ukrainians. Here, too, the Ukrainians were always far more advanced than the White Russians.

By the beginning of the twentieth century national aspirations had begun to clamor for recognition. After Poland was absorbed by Prussia, Austria, and Russia, the Poles became a minority group in each of these countries. It was only about 1904-1905 that the attitude of Russia toward minorities began to grow faintly more liberal. But a few years later, when the all-Russian Dumas began to function, the government reverted to an intolerant and oppressive policy towards its minorities. The ethnical minorities themselves tended to advocate autonomy, federation and full cultural self-determination. It was at that time, however, that the Russian National Rightists denied the national individuality of the Great Russians, who constituted 43 per cent of the population,[5] by adding to them the Ukrainians and the White Russians as two branches of the same Russian race.

After the first World War, the Ukrainians and the White Russians en-

5. The Ukrainians constituted 17 per cent of the population, the White Russians, 4.5 per cent. These figures based on the Russian census of 1897, which coincides roughly with the figures shown in the *Statistical Yearbook of Russia for 1915*, published by the Ministry of Internal Affairs. See Laserson, *The State Order and National Minorities*, p. 49.

joyed a brief period as independent states, following which these one-time satellites of Poland became satellites of Russia. Nevertheless, even after Soviet Russia had re-absorbed in 1921 the most important eastern areas of White Russia and the Ukraine, these two Slavonic peoples developed their own broad national autonomy and their own educational systems, including schools, universities and two academies of science, one in Minsk and the other in Kiev. The Soviet Union, however, continued to be apprehensive of all possible connections between Soviet White Russians and Ukrainians, and their kinsmen across the western borders which had been created by the Riga Treaty of 1921. The Soviet Union meticulously and generously supported the rights of both to cultural self-determination. However, all tendencies to local separation or to independent statehood were regarded as counter-revolutionary, or even as treachery towards the unity of the Soviet Union.

From this brief indication of the background, we may conclude that there is no single approach to the problem of the borderline between Poland and the Soviet Union. The attitude towards this question will vary according to the viewpoint of each of the ethnic groups concerned and their organs of political representation. We must therefore consider four approaches, those of the two states-nations, Poland and the Soviet Union, and those of the two dependent Slavic nations, the White Russians and the Ukrainians; and we must analyze each of these four approaches.

It would be tempting to simplify the whole problem by substituting legal interpretation of treaties and statements for a genuine consideration of all the deeper factors involved. Each litigant could then bring to court only those acts and documents, by nature or by interpretation favorable to his views, ignoring or weakening those of his opponent, with the judge of the court as the final arbiter. Many cases of litigation concerning frontier lines have been peacefully settled by such decisions and compromises.

But if the pressure of this war has evolved any new international principles, one of them is the second principle of the Atlantic Charter which states that "no territorial changes that do not accord with the freely expressed wishes of the peoples concerned" shall be carried out. This principle does away with the last remnants of the medieval conception of territory as a patrimonial right of the state. Populations are no longer considered as attached to the territories in which they live, and they are not now bound to the soil. Moreover, their wishes, freely expressed concerning the territory on which they live, constitute the deciding factor in any territorial changes. Whereas people were once the possession of the land, the land now is the possession of the people.

Of the four parties involved in the problem of the Russo-Polish frontier, two, Poland and the Soviet Union, are national states, with "co-national" kindred minorities in the areas under question, of which they are also neighbors on the west or on the east. The other two, the White Russians and the Ukrainians, are indigenous and the dominant ethnical population on the spot; for them the primary question remains their desire for full self-determination. For Poland and for Russia there are only two possible solutions: either to absorb the disputed territory or to allow it to be absorbed by the other. But for the White Russians and the Ukrainians there are three possibilities: to be absorbed by Russia, to be absorbed by Poland, or for each to form a national state of their own with the right to secede from any union.

All these questions were considered, and conclusions were reached, in 1919, during the discussions of the Supreme Council of the Allied and Associated Powers and its several commissions, particularly the Commission for the Investigation of Polish Affairs, the Interallied Commission at Warsaw, and others. The discussions, as well as the arguments presented at the Paris Peace Conference by the delegations of Poles, Ukrainians and White Russians, together with the results of the Russian Political Conference headed by the former Czarist Foreign Minister, Sazonov, covered approximately the same problems as are now on the agenda of the four interested parties.

It appears, from a conversation held March 19, 1919 in the Supreme Council[6] that there was a time when Poland and the Ukraine were considered almost equal claimants with regard to their territorial aspirations. By the middle of March, the war then going on between Poland and the Ukraine was reaching a critical stage because of the successes of the Ukrainians around Lwow, or Lemberg. Dr. Lord[7] set forth the proposal that the Conference send an urgent invitation to the Poles and the Ukrainians to agree to an immediate suspension of hostilities; that this suspension of hostilities be effected through a truce based substantially on the existing military *status quo,* but under conditions which would insure the security in Polish hands of the city of Lwow and of the railway connecting it with Przemysl. President Wilson observed that there were in Paris both Polish and Ukrainian representatives. It might perhaps be the quickest method if they were severally asked to inform their Governments that it was the desire of the Council that hostilities should cease and that if either party refused the truce its claims would not be heard by the Conference. Mr. Lloyd George pointed out[8] that the Conference hitherto had only heard the Poles. According to the maps he had, the majority of the population in Eastern

6. David Hunter Miller, *My Diary at the Conference of Paris* (1924), Vol. XV, pp. 411 ff.
7. Dr. Robert H. Lord was at that time member of the Inter-Allied Commission at Warsaw, representing the United States of America.
8. David Hunter Miller, *op. cit.,* Vol. XV, pp. 418, 419.

Galicia was Ukrainian. The country should, therefore, be attributed to them, unless very cogent reasons to the contrary existed. It was desirable, he stated, that the Conference should be strictly impartial. It was not improbable that what the Poles chiefly wanted in Eastern Galicia was the oilfields.

It was agreed that a telegram, signed by the heads of the delegations of the United States of America, the British Empire, France, Italy and Japan, should be sent to the Commanders-in-Chief of the Polish and Ukrainian forces with a request to conclude a truce immediately upon its receipt. The Supreme Council added that they were ready to hear the territorial claims of both parties concerned and to approach the Ukrainian and Polish Delegations in Paris, or whatever authorized representation the parties might select. Moreover, the hearing of the Ukrainian and Polish representatives with regard to their conflicting claims was made subject to the formal condition of immediate suspension of hostilities. Accordingly, a convention was concluded between the Polish and the Ukrainian armies.[9]

In an Annex, A-2, signed March 12, 1919 by Jules Cambon, there was presented to the same meeting of the Commission the statement that,

> It [the Commission for the Investigation of Polish Affairs] is at present studying the eastern frontiers, but is faced by the difficulty of ascertaining from what States Poland will be separated by these frontiers. . . .
>
> Mr. Sydorenko, President of the Delegation of the Ukraine Republic, has protested to the President of the Peace Conference against arrangements which would result in the separation of part of Galicia from the Ukraine. The Commission cannot ignore the fact that it would be difficult to come to a decision concerning the territorial claims of the Poles towards the East wtihout hearing the other side of the case.[10]

In the several Commissions there was certainly a tendency of benevolence toward Poland and an undeniable ideological hostility toward the young Soviet State.

In the Commission for the Investigation of Polish Affairs statements were made by delegates who arrived in Paris from Galicia, according to which

> the situation between the Poles and Ukrainians at Lwow has become critical, and the Poles are in danger of being defeated by the Ukrainians. . . . The loss of Lwow would have a tremendous effect throughout Poland and would be interpreted as a defeat of the Entente and as a victory of the Bolsheviks.

9. David Hunter Miller, *op. cit.*, Vol. XV, pp. 433-435.
10. *Ibid*, Vol. XVII, pp. 180-181.

On March 14, 1919, the same Commission submitted to the Supreme Council "the proposal to enjoin the Ukrainian Government, through the intermediary of the Warsaw Commission to accept an armistice."[11] This it did "with the object of making a simultaneous diplomatic attempt to save Lemberg [Lwow]."

Nevertheless, throughout all these discussions the ethnographical considerations were of prime importance. This was clear in an official conversation of the Foreign Ministers of the United States, Great Britain, France and Japan, held on April 26, 1919.[12] A note was drawn up and distributed, which stated as follows:

In regard to Eastern Galicia the Commission consider themselves at present debarred from making any definite recommendation as to the frontier in view of the decision taken by the Supreme Council at the meeting on the 19th March, 1919, that the Polish and Ukrainian Representatives should not be heard with regard to their respective claims in Eastern Galicia until the cessation of hostilities between the Polish and Ukrainian troops in that region.

In view of the constitution at Paris of an Interallied Commission to establish an armistice between the Polish and Ukrainian troops there appear to be grounds for hoping that a truce may be arranged in the near future, and accordingly, that it would be possible for the Commission to undertake the description of the frontier in Eastern Galicia.

Elsewhere, the Commission has been guided primarily by ethnic considerations[13] modified to a certain extent by various economic factors and the necessities of transport.

In regard to Galicia, however, if primarily ethnographical considerations were followed it is certain that in spite of the large Polish minority in Eastern Galicia the frontier of Poland would run west of Lemberg, [Lwow] unless an area containing a Ruthenian[14] majority were to be assigned to Poland.

This question thus introduces problems of general policy involving consequences of the utmost gravity. Several solutions may be considered, namely: the creation of an independent State, the establishment of an autonomous State under the control of the League of Nations, the partition of Eastern Galicia between Poland and the Ukraine. Either of these

11. David Hunter Miller, *op. cit.*, Vol. XVII, p. 182.

12. *Ibid.*, Vol. XVI, pp. 131-132. Also given in *Papers Relating to the Foreign Relations of the United States*, The Paris Peace Conference 1919, Washington, 1943. Vol. IV, pp. 624-625.

13. Italics ours.

14. "Ruthenian" is the old Austrian term for "Ukrainian." In the phrase "White Ruthenians" it is used to designate White Russians.

might, owing to the attraction which Russia would exercise upon a weak Slav State, result in the extension of the Russian frontier to the Carpathians.

On the other hand, it may be thought desirable to consider the political advantages which might result from the establishment of a common frontier between Poland and Rumania while securing for Eastern Galicia adequate guarantees in the way of local autonomy.

The Commission is of opinion that it is not possible to settle the frontiers of Poland in this region without determining at the same time the future status of Eastern Galicia. Considering that this question goes somewhat beyond its original mandate, the Commission respectfully approaches the Supreme Council with the request that it may be given:

Either explicit instructions as to the basis on which to carry out its work in this region, or a new mandate authorizing it to proceed with the study of this question.[15]

Beginning with the fall of 1919 it became apparent that on the part of the Allies there was a definite, growing inclination favoring Poland in the issue of the eastern boundary. The question of Eastern Galicia was discussed at two meetings of the Council of the Heads of Delegations, on September 19th and 25th. At these meetings the Council had before it the report of the Commission on Polish Affairs with regard to a proposed eastern boundary of Poland. The question was raised as to the form in which the Council intended to communicate these decisions. It was proposed to inform the Polish Government that the territories lying west of the line traced by the Commission[16] would definitely be attributed to Poland. It was decided to accept the report in question and to request the Drafting Committee to study and take the report as a basis for the means by which these decisions should be communicated to the Polish Government.[17]

From the time of the creation, within the framework of the Peace Conference, of the Commission for Poland, in January, 1919,[18] and all through the summer of the same year, hearings of Polish and Ukrainian representatives and the discussions and decisions upon questions of the eastern frontier of Poland were continuously postponed. On June 18, 1919, at the Meeting of the Foreign Ministers, M. Pichon of France said that the Council of Foreign Ministers had been asked by the Council of Four to find a definite settlement of the frontier between the Polish and the Ukrainian

15. See Chapter II, "The Character of the Polish Issue."

16. Later revised and designated the *Curzon Line*.

17. David Hunter Miller, *op. cit.*, Vol. XVI, pp. 538, 541, 542.

18. *Foreign Relations of the United States,* The Paris Peace Conference 1919, Washington, D. C., 1943. Vol. III, pp. 716-717.

territories.[19] Mr. Jules Cambon, the President of the Commission on Polish Affairs, could not explain what conclusions had been reached; he had not even consulted the members of his Commission, and therefore expressed only a personal opinion. But even this was but a kind of résumé based upon discussions in his Commission. These discussions turned upon two different viewpoints: those of The Right Honorable, A. J. Balfour (British Empire) and of H. E. Baron Sonnino (Italy).

As early as January 22, 1919, Mr. Balfour had developed a plan with a strong ethnographical approach to the whole problem, which he presented at the meeting of the Supreme War Council.[20] Eastern Galicia, according to the information at his disposal, did not desire to be Polish. He therefore suggested that "the Polish representatives should be gathered here and told that they must limit their actions to the protection of indisputable Polish territory against invasion from without. The ultimate frontiers of Poland should be left to the Peace Conference."

With this background, with the military clashes between the Ukraine and Poland not finally solved, with the growing danger of a Soviet-Polish war—which actually broke out the following summer,—and with a French attitude encouraging every kind of Polish aggrandizement, including the Ukrainian scheme, it is little wonder that the "final settlement of frontiers" was again postponed, in June, 1919.

At the historical meeting of June 18 Mr. Balfour advocated the idea of a provisional regime for Eastern Galicia the population of which was in his eyes "vigorously anti-Polish, and unwilling to be absorbed [by Poland]." The regime should be something between a mandate over Eastern Galicia, with a High Commissioner to be nominated by the future League of Nations, and a regime of Carpatho-Ruthenia to be attached to the Czecho-Slovak State. But, at the same time, Balfour regarded it "an abuse of the mandatory principle to give Poland the mandate." Sonnino defended some sort of autonomy for Galicia under Polish sovereignty. Mr. Lansing (United States of America) recognized that the Ukrainian (Ruthenian) population was 60 per cent illiterate, and therefore unfit for self-government. The occupation of Eastern Galicia by Polish troops should be only temporary, "until such time as the Great Powers might consider a plebiscite appropriate," when the question regarding ultimate sovereignty over the country would be solved. Lansing's proposal was in general accord with the project of Balfour. In contradistinction to the British plans, Cambon and Pichon maintained that a mandate should be conferred on Poland for the government of the country; and, after a discussion between Sonnino and Pichon,

19. *Ibid.*, Vol. IV, p. 828 ff. In the discussions the Commission on Polish Affairs is generally referred to as "Committee" or "Polish Committee."
20. *Ibid.*, Volume III, pp. 672-673.

it was pointed out that Lwow would be included in the territory attached to Poland.

But still no final settlement of frontiers was reached, neither at the Peace Conference nor, as a consequence, by the Treaty of Versailles. On Dec. 8, 1919 the Supreme Council suggested a provisional eastern frontier for Poland. It was only in the summer of 1920, after the invasion by the Polish armies of the Russian Ukraine proper, that the Curzon Line emerged as a sort of geographical boundary between the three Slavic entities: Poland, the Ukraine and Russia. At the Spa Conference, on July 10, Mr. Lloyd George interviewed Mr. Grabski, the representative of Poland. He asked the Poles to withdraw some 125 miles behind the line which they at that time occupied, on Russian and Ukrainian territory. This would bring them to their "legitimate frontier." Mr. Grabski inquired where that frontier lay. Mr. Lloyd George then indicated what has since been known as the Curzon Line,"[21] that is, a line running from somewhat north of Grodno, south through Bialystok, Brest-Litovsk and Przemysl, to the Carpathians. Mr. Grabski expressed dissent, whereupon Mr. Lloyd George assured him that if the Poles retired to the Curzon Line, and if the Russians subsequently crossed it, then "the British Government and their Allies would be bound to help Poland with all the means at their disposal."

On July 20 Lord Curzon addressed a communication to Moscow in which he made it clear that the Allies would come to the aid of Poland if the Russian forces crossed the Curzon Line. This was the first appearance of the Line in international negotiations, but it was without any immediate practical results at that time, because, first, the Line was crossed by the Russians four days later, and then, in the Riga Treaty of March, 1921,[22] it was ignored by both the Russians and the Poles. Now, twenty-five years later, in the last phase of the second World War, the Curzon Line is occupying a prominent place on the international forum.

21. See Harold Nicolson, *Curzon: the Last Phase 1910-1925*, New York, 1939, pp. 204-205.
22. League of Nations Treaty Series, Vol. VI, p. 123.

2. Poland

APPROACHED from the standpoint of Poland, the question of the Curzon Line has presented many difficult and complex problems, as a result of which a number of Polish parties and movements have been formed, offering different solutions, most of which reach far into the general political problem of the reconstruction of Poland.

THE CHARACTER OF THE POLISH ISSUE

The starting point for this, as for all other elements of the question, is the period of the first World War and the peace settlements, or from 1916 to the conclusion of the Riga Peace Treaty on March 18, 1921. Important milestones mark these intermediary years. Among them there was in the first place, on November 5, 1916, the imperial German and Austro-Hungarian proclamation of the future independence of Poland. This was followed by the proclamation of a free Poland by Imperial Russia on December 25, 1916, on the eve of the Kerensky revolution. Then a month later came the address of President Wilson to the United States Senate in which he said, "I take it for granted . . . that statesmen everywhere are agreed that there should be a united, independent, and autonomous Poland." Later, on January 8, 1918, came President Wilson's Fourteen Points, with the guarantee of Polish independence, in terms which took note of the ethnographical factor, as follows:

> An independent Polish State should be erected which should include the territories inhabited by indisputably Polish populations, which should be assured a free and secure access to the sea, and whose political and economic independence and territorial integrity should be guaranteed by international covenant.

The independence of Poland was recognized by Russia, under Kerensky, on March 30, 1917,[1] and by Soviet Russia on August 29, 1918, according to the decree of the Council of the People's Commissars. Finally, the recognition of the restored sovereignty of Poland was assured by the Versailles

---

1. The Monitor of the Provisional Government, No. 11/57, 1917.

Treaty, on June 28, 1919, signed by Poland and the United States, Great Britain, France, Italy and Japan. The concluding touch was given by the Riga Treaty of 1921, at the end of the war between Soviet Russia and Poland, which for the first time delimited the frontier between the neighboring states. This frontier was recognized March 15, 1923, by the Conference of Ambassadors representing the United States, the British Empire, France, Italy and Japan. Acquiescing in this settlement, the Conference withdrew the proposal for a mandate over Eastern, or Ukrainian, Galicia which originally had been allotted to Poland for twenty-five years, after which the whole question of Eastern Galicia was to have been re-opened by the League of Nations. This "betrayal of trust," as the Ukrainians termed it, was thus not an act of the League but of the Conference of Ambassadors.

Although the old Polish intransigent dream of restoring the borders of 1772 did not materialize, nevertheless Poland was recognized widely beyond her ethnographic boundaries. The borders proposed to Poland by the Soviets in April, 1920, in order to stop the war, were even more favorable for Poland than those fixed in the Riga Peace Treaty.[2] Until the autumn of 1939, the western part of White Russia and the western parts of the Ukraine, including Eastern Galicia and the most western section of Volhynia, remained under the domination of Poland.

Radical chauvinistic claims to the contrary, the fact is that restored Poland was territorially satisfied both in the west against Germany and in the east against the Soviet Union.

Moreover, through the years between 1921 and 1939, a kind of stabilized equilibrium was achieved which confirmed the territorial borders between Poland and the Soviet Union. On July 25, 1932, Poland and the Soviet Union signed a treaty of non-aggression.[3] In the preamble to this treaty, the Treaty of Riga (1921) was reaffirmed. Under Article I each party pledged itself to abstain from "any act of violence attacking the integrity and inviolability of territory or the political independence" of the other. According to Article 3 each of the signatories undertook "not to be a party to any agreement openly hostile to the other." On July 3, 1933, a convention for the Definition of Aggression was signed between the U.S.S.R. and her neighbors, Afghanistan, Estonia, Latvia, Persia, Poland, Rumania and Turkey.[4] According to Article 2 any state invading "by armed forces, even without a declaration of war, the territory of another State" is to be considered an aggressor. On May 5, 1934, the Treaty of Non-Aggression between Poland and the U.S.S.R., which had been signed on July 25, 1932, was renewed

2. This is officially admitted by the *Great Soviet Encyclopaedia*, Volume 46, p. 247.
3. League of Nations Treaty Series, Vol. 86, p. 41.
4. Max M. Laserson, "The Development of Soviet Foreign Policy in Europe, 1917-1942," in *International Conciliation*, 1943, No. 386, p. 64-65.

until December 31, 1945. Among the declarations and statements relating to Soviet-Polish relations was that made by Mr. Litvinov on February 14, 1934, at a reception given in honor of the Polish Foreign Minister, Colonel Beck, when he referred to the excellent relationship existing between Russia and Poland and to "the profound process of rapprochement" between them. It was only as late as August 31, 1939, at the session of the Supreme Soviet dedicated to the ratification of the Soviet-German pact of August 23, 1939, that Mr. Molotov changed his tone towards Poland, stating that Poland's attitude had been taken "according to the instructions of England and France."[5]

It goes without saying that any succession Polish government, however liberal, would lean heavily on the achievements of 1921 and their sanctioning by usage throughout a score of years. That is what the Government-in-exile did. Such an attitude is natural to a state which has enjoyed undisputed stability in its foreign relations; but with a country like Poland, restored after a hundred and twenty years of absorption and hostile domination by foreign powers, it is even more understandable. It was natural, then, that with this tendency to hold on to all her territories, Poland tried to ignore ethnographic issues. She had had some sort of federation with Lithuania and White Russia in the north since the fourteenth century, and for a long period with the Ukrainians in the south. The bonds of her federation depended upon dynastic ties, and the union was a loosely knit combination of various upper classes, all of them with some tendency to Polonization. Under these medieval conditions the non-Polish population exhibited no political consciousness whatever.[6]

But with the nineteenth century came new political affinities. White Russians and Ukrainians grew more conscious of their existence as individual nations—of their own "place in the sun." This historic development was by no means confined to Poland. It was taking place, simultaneously, in other multi-national countries wherever the abolition of serfdom and the consequent improvement of social conditions had led to national self-determination and political maturity. All peasant minorities, and especially those in absolutist Russia, Austria-Hungary and Turkey, were following this trend. So long as Poland was partitioned and under the domination of three foreign powers, the Poles could scarcely be very conscious of ethnographic

5. *Ibid.,* p. 33.

6. It is significant that in Polish Government circles there are those who do not perceive the seriousness of the situation as a whole. They do not understand that with the Polish people independence comes first, territorial integrity in the second place. In an article on "Postwar Poland," the well-known historian, Oscar Halecki, argues that the establishment of the Curzon Line as a boundary would take Poland "back six hundred years, to the first half of the fourteenth century," despite the fact, which he himself admits, that "without real independence, the problem of territorial integrity becomes meaningless." *(Slavonic and East European Review,* Wisconsin, May 1944, pp. 28-40).

differences, although these had actually been developing in their country for centuries. In their common fight against the Russian Czarist regime, as the oppressor of all minorities, these differences had become somewhat blurred, and even the Fourteen Points and the shaping of the Curzon Line caused no change in the traditional attitude.

But when Poland was faced with the opportunity of again becoming a Polish state, ethnical differences suddenly became apparent. In Imperial Austria, which had many more democratic institutions and bodies of local self-government, this consciousness of difference came less abruptly. Eastern Galicia, which belonged to Austria, had been for decades a much more open and active field of clashes between Poles and Ukrainians than the Russian-owned territory in the extreme western section of Volhynia, in the Lutsk area, where Poles and Ukrainians also were living side by side.

Foreign Relations

Another factor which increased the complexity of the Polish issue was the character of her foreign relations. The new Poland was not only more handicapped than other states because of being less homogeneous, it had also a far worse geographical situation than the Netherlands, the Scandinavian states, Finland or even the Baltic States, all of which possessed the advantage of being on the outskirts of Europe.

The new Poland, by the mere fact of geography, was immediately sandwiched in between Germany and Russia, as it had been for centuries, with the difference, however, that in the preceding century Germany had grown to be a great united military power. Thus, with the restoration of Poland, the old struggle for the balance of power was resumed. Had the new family of nations been based on principles opposed to the traditional doctrine and practice of power politics, the political rebirth of Poland might have proved of no particular significance. But the new regime of the League of Nations failed to control the old-line forces of the eighteenth century which had led to Poland's obliteration in 1795. Internationalism, as practised by the League, tolerated full national sovereignty, so that old ties and friendships, inherited from the former system of balance of power, were merely renewed by the nations in question.

It was only natural, therefore, that whatever Poland's internal regime might be, her resurrection was regarded with especially friendly eyes by France. For France this was merely the return of her historic ally, for whom Czarist Russia had, from the nineties on, been substituted. From the time of Richelieu if not earlier, with an interruption during the days of Napoleon III, France had pursued the policy of balancing the Central European powers by means of alliances on the Eastern frontiers. Poland was usually prominent among these allies, both while she was a sovereign state and later when she was revolting against her reactionary dominators, Prussia, Russia and Austria, a revolt in which she was supported by France. The military help given by France to Poland against the invading Soviet armies in 1920 was the best possible beginning for a new period of friendship and alliance. On February 18, 1921, shortly before the conclusion of the Riga Treaty with the Soviets, a definite treaty of alliance was signed between France and Poland. This alliance was bound to come about, regardless of the type of government in Poland.

The Franco-Polish alliance held firm till Hitler seized power in the beginning of 1933. At this time Marshal Pilsudski secretly proposed that France should engage in a preventive war against Germany, but nothing materialized from his proposal. Poland had, since 1926, been living under the rather reactionary and semi-dictatorial regime of a military oligarchy, and now for the sake of her own security she made a complete turn-about in her foreign policy. The result was the Polish-German non-aggression agreement of January 27, 1934.[7] It was not until just before the outbreak of the second World War and Germany's attack on Poland that the reactionary Polish government, until then entirely subservient to Hitler Germany, suddenly began to try to re-align itself with the West. An Anglo-Polish Agreement for assistance was signed on August 25, 1939.[8] Under Article 1, Great Britain pledged herself to give "all the support and assistance in her power" if Poland were to become engaged in hostilities with a European power in consequence of aggression by the latter. Needless to say, Britain honored her pledge on September 3, 1939, by going to war with Germany.

The Minorities Problem

From this short survey of international political issues it is evident that Poland's allies never made a request or a serious demand that she observe the ethnographical borders between herself and her Slavic minorities in the east. Indeed, the decision of the 1923 Conference of Ambassadors to abolish the autonomy of Eastern Galicia was a step in quite the opposite direction. Moreover, from the viewpoint of traditional French policy, Poland made a better balance as a buffer state if her territory remained larger and her general population greater. If the areas east of the Curzon Line were separated from Poland, it would diminish her territory by about one-half

7. *Official Documents Concerning Polish-German and Polish-Soviet Relations, 1933-1939; Polish White Book,* Published by the authorization of the Polish Government, Hutchinson, London. Document No. 10.

8. *Ibid.,* Document No. 91. For full text see, *Agreement between the Government of the United Kingdom and the Polish Government Regarding Mutual Assistance;* Poland No. 1, (1945), Cmd. 6616.

and her population by a third.[9] The only detailed bilateral agreement concerning one of her minority groups entered into by Poland was that signed in Geneva on May 5, 1922, between Poland and Germany, relating to the German minority in Upper Silesia.

In the Minorities Treaty which Poland signed on June 28, 1919,[10] no specific mention was made of her Slavic minorities, but merely a general admission of the existence in Poland of racial, religious, and linguistic minorities, to whom certain rights were granted by an elementary bill of rights, including instruction in the primary schools in their own respective languages. All minorities were also assured of an equitable share in the enjoyment and application of grants from the public funds of the state, or from municipal budgets for educational, religious, and charitable work. No possibility of territorial autonomy for Galicia or any other area was mentioned. The rights of Jews to have their own communities, educational committees and schools, and to observe the Jewish Sabbath were included. The German minority was mentioned only for a matter of limitation, the statement being that minority rights "shall apply to Polish citizens of German speech, only in that part of Poland which was German territory in August, 1914," or before the outbreak of the first World War. It should be noted also that minority, religious and educational rights were granted to the respective minorities by the Peace Treaty of Riga in 1921, in Article 7 of which Russian Ukrainians and Russians were mentioned as national minorities. This treaty, however, does not belong in the category of so-called minorities treaties.

But even though international treaties and alliances had included no agreements binding Poland to preserve any important rights for her minorities, voluntary legislation within Poland itself could have achieved a still more positive result. Certain minority rights, it is true, were granted by the Constitution of March 17, 1921,[11] particularly in Articles 95, 109, 110, 111, but at no time were these Articles put into practice by special organic legislation. They remained merely solemn promises. In Poland's new and semi-Fascist Constitution of April 23, 1935[12] the section on civic rights and duties was reduced, with the exception of the minority articles 109, 110 and 111,

9. The Curzon Line does not fully coincide with the line of Soviet-German demarcation of September 28, 1939. It deviated farther to the west both in Eastern Galicia and in the Bialystok northern area (see map). The Soviet-German demarcation line, which is less favorable for Poland, cuts from Poland, according to official Polish figures, 51.6 per cent of her territory and 37.3 per cent of the total population. Cf. *Polish Facts and Figures*, No. 2, March, 1944, New York.

10. British Treaty Series (1919), No. 8, Cmd. 223.

11. H. L. McBain and L. Rogers: *The New Constitutions of Europe;* New York City, 1923; chapter 16.

12. Stanislaw Car: *Constitution of the Republic of Poland of 1935:* Polish Commission for International Law Co-operation, Warsaw, 1935.

which were retained partly in order not openly to violate her Minority Treaty and partly because three million Germans were still living in Polish territory, and Poland, having made her sudden shift of foreign policy, had signed a pact in January, 1934, with Hitler's Germany.[13]

Although Pilsudski's original plans went far toward recognizing territorial autonomy for White Russia and East Galicia, the plans did not materialize. Keen opposition to them began to show itself in the first years of Poland's independence. Pilsudski's plan, which was to encourage national self-government in both these border states, had behind it the idea of using them as buffer states between Poland and the Soviet Union. Ironically enough, exactly the reverse now seems likely to take place, since both these border provinces will probably be absorbed by the Soviet Union, or rather by the Soviet Republics of White Russia and the Ukraine.

Poland did not even give to her border provinces the same autonomous recognition which she herself had enjoyed under the dual monarchy of Austria-Hungary. Under Polish domination no official Ukrainian or White Russian universities were established, despite the fact that such universities and schools, and even academies of science, existed on the other side of the Polish-Soviet border. Profiting from her own experience in the years preceding 1914 when Russian and Prussian Poles, persecuted and discriminated against on cultural lines, had looked to Austrian Poland as a kind of "Piedmont" on which they concentrated their national aspirations and dreams, the new Poland should have come to an understanding with her own minorities. Instead she estranged the White Russians and the Ukrainians, and indirectly encouraged the majority population of her eastern provinces to turn with longing toward the Soviet East.

Even before the harsh punitive measures of "violent pacification" which the Polish government adopted against Ukrainian Galicia in 1930-1931, and against White Russian peasantry even earlier, a state of great tension had developed in the eastern provinces. The only social difference between the peasantry of these provinces and the people of the Soviet Union was that, being small property owners, they objected to compulsory collectivization. To Ukrainians on a lower level, with no property at all, not even this objection was valid; and, for them all, what the Ukrainians and White Russians on the other side of the border had achieved in national culture was an undeniable fact.

It is this situation that explains the reasons behind the positive results of the Soviet plebiscite in Eastern Poland in October, 1939. Unquestionably

13. On September 13, 1934, Colonel Beck declared to the League of Nations that his Government was compelled to refuse all further co-operation with that international organization in the supervision of the application by Poland of the system of national minority protection.

the methods of the Soviet occupational authorities permitted no expression of free will on the part of the people. The election committees were packed with Russian officials and members of the secret police; the polling was conducted with ballots bearing the name of only one candidate; and all these manoeuvers were carried out under cover of the bayonets of armed occupational forces. It was in no way a democratic election or an impartial plebiscite. But one has every reason to believe that even had the voting been fairly conducted the final results of the plebiscite would scarcely have favored a Polish sovereignty, except in towns like Lwow (Lemberg) and their surrounding areas where there was a clear Polish majority.

All this sufficiently explains the behavior of the Government-in-exile, except for the radical rightists and the pro-Soviet opposition. In the "official" attitude one finds reflected the character of the Polish issue itself. Poland's legal claim was based on the Riga Peace Treaty and the Versailles Treaty, and upon her subsequent two decades of independence when the *status quo* of her borders was left undisturbed. Legally, therefore, Poland was a victim of aggressive attack from the west by Germany and of invasion from the east by the Soviet Union. Until September, 1939, she had been the "blessed possessor." No one except Germany had ever denied the legality of her borders, and the Soviet Union had raised no diplomatic objections concerning her ethnographic purity. None of the declarations, including the Fourteen Points, ever stated that ethnical homogeneity was an essential for founding a sovereign state, or questioned whether a multiethnical state, if it emerged, should be recognized. Many other such states made up of ethnical mixtures were already in existence near Poland.

Moreover, Poland's own history—her union with Lithuania and her cooperation with the old Ukrainian Cossack Republic—had made no demands upon her to revise the constitution of her state. It is true that, as mentioned earlier, in Poland's formative years from 1918 to 1921, diplomatic objections and requests made to the Supreme Council in the Peace Conference by White Russians and Ukrainians, and even formal military action and war on their part, had proved clearly enough the spirit of resistance and the national aspirations of these two peoples. But so long as Poland's borders, which comprised various territorial minorities, were established and recognized by the family of nations, she remained legally sovereign, and each new protest from a minority was consequently regarded as subversive action if not open treason.

The Polish Government-in-exile, deprived of territory by Germany's invasion and occupation, continued to assert its legal right to possession. All other issues might be open to question but this legal status, sanctioned by international law and by diplomatic agreement, remained the one undeniable and immovable rock in a welter of uncertainty.

Poland's former *status quo* had been somewhat undermined, at least in the eyes of her opponents, by Germany's aggression and by the treaty of non-aggression between Germany and Soviet Russia on August 23, 1939, as well as by other conventions concerning the borders of German and Soviet domination in Poland. However, after the agreement of July 30, 1941 was concluded between the U.S.S.R. and the Polish Government, according to which "the government of the U.S.S.R. recognized the Soviet-German treaties of 1939 concerning territorial changes in Poland as having lost their validity,"[14] Poland's rights appeared to have been completely restored.

POLISH PARTIES AND GROUPS

In the exiled Polish circles supporting the Government-in-exile little if any friction developed concerning national policies, least of all concerning problems of the Eastern frontiers of the Poland of the future. If a radical opposition to the views of the government, especially relating to the Eastern frontiers, did exist, it was found in two directly opposing groups, the Communists and the Rightists, though the latter gave fuller support after M. Arciszewski became Premier. Opposition was also to be found in Polish circles with a pro-Soviet tendency. Among those groups which supported the Government, there were only slight differences of opinion.

In March 1943 the Polish Government was made up of the following:

1. Two members of the Peasant Party, an agrarian populist group with a democratic background;
2. Two members of the Socialist Party;
3. Two members of the National Democratic Party, both reactionary Conservatives;
4. Two members of the Christian Polish Labor Party (clerical-Catholic);
5. Five non-party members, among them Sikorski himself, and General Kukiel.

After the death of Prime Minister Sikorski a political shift to the left brought about basic changes in the Cabinet. Instead of two representatives from each of the Leftist Parties, Socialist and Peasant, the new Cabinet had three members from each, among them, as Prime Minister, Mikolajczyk, who belongs to the Peasant Party. The National Democrats and the Polish Labor Party each retained two seats as before. The number of non-party members was reduced from five to three, among them General Kukiel as

14. *New York Times,* July 31, 1941.

Minister of Defense,[15] and Tadeusz Romer, Minister of Foreign Affairs. The posts of Vice-Prime Minister, held by Kwapinski; Minister of Labor and Social Welfare, held by Stanczyk; and Finance Minister, held by Grossfeld, all went to the Socialist Party. The President, Raczkiewicz, and the former Commander-in-Chief, General Sosnkowski, belonged to the OZON group, the party of Pilsudski.

The leaders of that part of the Polish left which supported the Government-in-exile were in practical agreement on Russo-Polish relations. Marcyn Rylski, a prominent Polish Socialist, in his article on Poland and Russia—see the *Nation* of October 9, 1943—stressed the unity on this issue. The article read in part as follows:

> Indeed, it is a question which transcends the boundaries of parties, as the Foreign Committee of the Polish Socialist Party in London openly acknowledged in a resolution adopted on June 30, 1943: "In the present conflict between Poland and the Soviet Union the attitude of all Polish groups is similar. Any assertion that there is a split between Polish democracy and Polish reaction on this matter represents the interference of foreign elements in Polish internal affairs—and we reject such interference resolutely."

Rylski went on to insist upon the old *status quo* of 1921-1939, as opposed to ethnographical considerations:

> The official policy of the leadership of the Polish Labour movement and the Polish Peasant Party in London upholds the integrity of the Polish frontiers of 1939. It denies the Soviet thesis that the Eastern portions of Poland, occupied in 1939 by the Red Army, belong to the Soviet Union as integral parts of the Ukrainian, White Russian, and Lithuanian Soviet Republics.

The Soviet and the Polish Governments had stated their respective positions many times:

> It is undeniable that the territories in question—especially if some rectifications of boundaries are made—have Ukrainian and White Russian majorities, the Poles constituting an important minority. But the Polish boundaries established by the peace treaty signed at Riga in 1921, ending the Polish War, aroused no debate for eighteen years. The Polish government wants to re-establish those boundaries.

In this same resolution of June 30, 1943, the Polish Socialist Party stated that all those holding an opposing opinion on the Russo-Soviet question had automatically placed themselves outside the Polish Socialist Party.

15. *Novy Swiat,* a New York Polish Daily, July 15, 1943.

Among those expelled by this resolution were the group of Polish Democrats and Socialists in the United States headed by Professor Oscar Lange, and some of the political and union leaders among the Polish Americans. Groups of similar tendencies exist in Britain. After New York, London is the second and Moscow the third most important center of Polish emigrants favoring a pro-Soviet movement, in opposition to the views of their Government-in-exile. It is in Moscow that the League of Polish Patriots headed by Wanda Wasilewska, former member of the Polish Socialist Party, has had its center.

Like the Polish emigrants, the members of the one-time Polish Underground have also been divided on this question, and discussions, disputes and even fighting have occurred in underground groups.

Opposing the Government-in-exile were the following Right wing groups:

1. The Right Wing of the National Democrats which before the war had a pro-Hitler and a strong anti-Semitic tendency;

2. The National Radical Camp, the O.N.R., who are even more rightist than the National Democrats;

3. The National Union Camp, the OZON, which was organized by Colonel Koc and is composed of Pilsudski followers.

The Rightist opposition publishes an organ, *Mysl Polska (The Polish Thought)*, which is definitely anti-Soviet. The majority of the National Democrats belong to this opposition. It is significant that the two members of their party who entered the Cabinet-in-exile—M. Seyda as the Minister to prepare *pourparlers* for the peace, and Professor Komarnicki, as Minister of Justice—were both subsequently expelled from the National Democratic Party. All the followers of the late Marshal Pilsudski are among the opposition groups, mostly with OZON, the National Union Camp, and are permanently affiliated with the National Democrats. Whether or not the National Democrats in the one-time Underground supported the Government-in-exile, is still difficult to ascertain.

In the United States the Rightist opposition to the Polish Government is led by the Daily *Novy Swiat*, whose leading writer is Ignacy Matuszewski. Although not very outspoken, this newspaper has clearly opposed the proposal of the Government to declare the Curzon Line a provisional basis for future negotiations for a permanent boundary with the Soviet Union; it opposed co-operation with the Russian Army in Poland, viewing the Government's proposal so to co-operate as a political error; and, following the last Soviet-Czechoslovak Treaty, it demanded that the Government-in-exile break off diplomatic relations with Czechoslovakia.

The whole Rightist opposition in general is against ceding one inch of the Polish territory assigned by the Riga Treaty. The Rightists consider the Government's proposal to use the Curzon Line as a basis for negotiations almost an act of treachery. They have made many attempts, especially in London and during the San Francisco Conference, to enlist sympathy for their anti-Soviet stand. This Rightist opposition naturally has a social and political influence on certain very important elements of the Polish Army formerly under the command of General Sosnkowski. Although the assertion made by the Soviet organ, *The War and the Working Class*, in October, 1943, that there are two Polish governments, one civil and one military, may be regarded as an exaggeration, it is true that tension does exist between the Government-in-exile and the Polish Army.

The Leftist Opposition included certain independent groups of Socialists and Democrats, some Polish and some now American citizens who have tried to get the Government-in-exile to compromise with the Soviet Union. In the Soviet Union itself there is a Union of Polish Patriots, sometimes referred to as the League of Polish Patriots, whose attitude is almost identical with the official view of the Soviet Government. Contact was established in 1943 between the independent opposition and the League of Polish Patriots by the visits of Professor Lange and the Rev. Stanislaw Orlemanski to the Soviet Union.

As mentioned earlier, the independent opposition in the United States has been led by Professor Lange, formerly of the University of Cracow, now a professor in the University of Chicago. On October 5, 1943, Professor Lange published, in the *New York Herald Tribune,* a letter entitled "Poland's Place in the Post-War World," which clearly outlined his political views. We quote from him as follows:

> In order that Poland be prosperous and a factor of stability in Europe she must have a democratic form of government and an agrarian reform which will eliminate the feudal elements in the country by giving the land to the peasants. Poland must also have a frontier with Germany which will enable her to serve effectively as a bulwark of defense against German aggression toward any nation in Eastern Europe (including the Soviet Union). Poland's pre-war frontier did not satisfy this condition. . . . Poland should have all of Upper Silesia with a prevailingly Polish population. Since the Polish population there consists of peasants and workers, while the upper classes are German, this will be a step toward social democracy. . . .
>
> Further, a democratic Poland should be guaranteed sovereignty over East Prussia (except for a small part of it, which is inhabited by Lithuanians). This demand cannot be fully supported on ethnographic grounds. However, a large section of the population of East Prussia is still Polish-

speaking (the Mazurians) and an even larger part has been Germanified so recently that it would revert to Polish Nationality under the mere influence of the new political environment (without any coercion). Polish sovereignty over East Prussia is necessary for the peace of Europe. East Prussia is the land of the Junkers, the breeding-ground of Prussian militarism. . . . Both for social and for national reasons a democratic Poland will have to expropriate the Junkers, to ship them out of the country and to settle their estates with peasants. This will break once and for all the social basis of Prussian militarism.

As to the eastern borders of Poland, and particularly in connection with an improved Curzon Line, Professor Lange makes the following proposals:

A final prerequisite for Poland's future is an amicable solution of the boundary dispute with the Soviet Union. The Polish nation must recognize the right of the Ukrainians and White Ruthenians to national reunion with the Soviet Ukraine and Soviet White Ruthenia. Attempts to force these peoples into Poland against their will can result only (as it has in the past) in a weakening of the Polish state by internal dissension. Furthermore, the coercion which this would require is incompatible with the effective operation of democracy in Poland. . . . On the other hand, the Soviet Government should recognize the existence of ancient centers of Polish culture (such as the City Lwow, for instance)[16] which, though situated in ethnographically Ukrainian or White Ruthenian territory, form such an integral part of Polish national life that they cannot be separated from Poland without serious detriment to the friendly relations between the Polish and the Soviet people. To the Ukrainian and White Ruthenian people these centers mean very little, their real cultural centers being in places like Kiev, Kharkov, Minsk and others. Leaving these centers with Poland would separate from the Soviet Union a relatively small number of Ukrainians and White Ruthenians, who would be granted full national freedom by a democratic Poland. Such an arrangement would bring abundant rewards to the Ukrainian and White Ruthenian peoples as well as to the whole Soviet Union by a true and lasting friendship of the Polish people.

Professor Lange's letter was criticized by New York's Ukrainian Bi-Weekly, *Gromadski Golos,* in October, 1943, especially his demand that, despite ethnographic considerations, centers like Lwow or Vilna and their surrounding districts should remain under Polish domination. It was sug-

16. Professor Lange avoids citing another ancient center similar to Lwow. But obviously when mentioning a center situated in White Ruthenian territory, he has in mind Vilna, or Vilnius, which was demanded by Lithuanians as far back as 1919.

gested that Professor Lange apply to the Ukrainian districts with a Polish nobility as landowners the same yardstick he would apply to Polish peasants and workers living in Eastern Prussia under the German Junkers; in other words, that the Polish nobles of Eastern Poland be dispossessed and their estates divided among the Ukrainian peasants.

UNION OF POLISH PATRIOTS

The Union of Polish Patriots was established in the U.S.S.R. in June or July of 1943 and, according to its weekly organ, *Wolna Polska,* of December 31, 1943, the Union celebrated its first half year of existence that December. The fact of its establishment and its connection with the Polish Army corps was officially admitted by the Soviet Government's declaration of January 11, 1944. It reads in part:

> In this war of liberation, the Union of Polish Patriots in the U.S.S.R. and the Polish army corps created by it and operating on the front against the Germans, hand in hand with the Red Army, are already fulfilling their gallant tasks.[17]

At the head of the Union was Wanda Wasilewska, a well known Polish writer who was formerly a member of the Polish Socialist Party but who, after the defeat of Poland, joined the Communist Party of the U.S.S.R. With her were other leaders, among them Andrej Witos, formerly a member of the radical Peasant Party, and a relative of the famous democratic Polish statesman. Other important members of the Union of Polish Patroits were former adherents of the Polish Socialist Party, like Boleslaw Drobner, founder of the Independent Socialist Party, who was close to Communist views. In the membership lists of the Union of Polish Patriots and in those of the first Polish army corps, where previous party affiliations are indicated, may also be noted former reactionaries, some from the Catholic group, and others from the National Democrats and from the most consistent followers of Pilsudski.

The Union and the Army Corps have passed resolutions against the Government-in-exile and against regarding the Polish National Council in London as a representative parliament. One of these resolutions, published in *Wolna Polska* on December 31, 1943, described the London Council as incapable of representing the interests of the Polish people, and charged the Council and its leaders with "co-operation with our enemy, Hitler, for the purpose of establishing Fascism in Poland."

There is no doubt that the Union of Polish Patriots has greatly helped to

17. *The Foreign Policy of the Soviet Union during the War for the Fatherland,* (Russian): Moscow, 1944, Vol. 1, p. 129.

organize and unify the hundreds of thousands of Poles left in Russia after the Polish disaster, and improved their living conditions. The Union was also an aid to the Polish army which was, at that time, a fighting unit under Soviet command.

The bi-weekly, *Nowe Widnokregi (New Horizons)*, another important Polish-Soviet organ, is an interesting combination of pro-Soviet and pro-Slavic opinion. It has given considerable importance to the idea of the unity of Eastern Slavs, particularly Russians, Poles, Ukrainians and White Russians. With this in view it culls the history of past centuries and publishes many historical articles with illustrations showing the historic landmarks of Poland, the Ukraine and the like.

Although the independent Leftist opposition has had recent contacts with Moscow and a cordial reception at the Kremlin, for our consideration it should not be confused with the Union of Polish Patriots. The Union was a political organization of Poles left in the Soviet Union after the defeat of September, 1939, and the evacuation of the Polish Army, followed by a mass deportation of Polish civilians into the U.S.S.R. The Union was not against an independent Poland. It demanded a parliamentary democracy and extensive agrarian and economic changes but at the same time it advocates a continuing alliance between Poland and the U.S.S.R., though whether this should be a loose international alliance or a close confederation between the two countries is not entirely clear. The Union and its activities might therefore have been included in our chapter devoted to "The Soviet Approach." However, since it was a patriotic Polish organization, consisting of people who were keenly aware of their Polish nationality, it proved to be an important political factor as the Polish Soviet army divisions and the Union marched together into Poland.

In a report made by responsible officers concerning the motives and intentions of the Union Soviet Army,[18] it was stated that the Union of Polish Patriots was only temporary and would make no attempt to become the new Polish government. "We know," its spokesman said, "that if we went home with a ready-made Government the people would be against it. What we intend to do is to see that no fascist regime is established and that a Government is found that recognizes the necessity of getting along with Soviet Russia."

BEFORE AND AFTER THE RUPTURE OF DIPLOMATIC RELATIONS

The situation as described above remained unchanged for some time. During the first months after the conclusion of the treaty of July 30, 1941, in which the question of Eastern Poland was not mentioned, diplomatic

18. See *New York Times*, March 30, 1944; a despatch from Moscow.

relations between Poland and Russia were smooth and cloudless. However, in February, 1943, they took a turn for the worse. In the treaty of July, 1941, the U.S.S.R. had consented to the formation on its territory "of a Polish army under a commander appointed by the Polish Government in agreement with the Soviet Government."[19] This army was recruited mainly from deported Polish citizens within the zone of Soviet occupation in the autumn of 1939. On August 14, 1941, a military agreement[20] was concluded between the U.S.S.R. and Poland. The recruiting for the army met with considerable success; by February 1942, its divisions included 73,415 men. Further negotiations provided that it should not be bound to any maximum limit. But despite British and American help the supplying and arming of the newly formed companies was rendered extremely difficult by the complications of transport, difficulties which steadily increased. A second military agreement was signed on January 22, 1942, providing that the Polish army be raised to 96,000 men with equipment, but this agreement did not materialize.

In February, 1942, five months after the formation of Polish units began, the Soviet Government pointed out that the Fifth Polish Division had completed its training and asked when it would go into action. According to the seventh article of the Soviet-Polish military agreement of August 14, 1941, "Polish Army units [were to] be moved to the front upon achievement of full fighting readiness." It is true that some of the men were not fully equipped according to the standards established for the Polish Army in Great Britain, but their situation was similar to that of many Russian troops. General Anders, Polish Commander in Russia, repeatedly delayed sending his troops to the front on the ground that the six divisions being planned should all go at the same time. The agreement of 1941, however, only provided that "Polish soldiers will march out as a rule in formations not smaller than a division and will be used in conformity with the plan of operations of the Supreme Command of the U.S.S.R." As Poles were fighting on other fronts, in units as small as brigades, it became clear that General Anders did not want to use his troops on the Soviet-German front.

In fact, General Anders made such a gloomy report to Churchill on the impossibility of Russian resistance that the latter was won over to the idea of evacuating Polish troops from Russia and also transferred large numbers of Indian troops from Burma to Iraq and Persia to meet the German advance which Anders predicted after the Russian collapse.

In March, 1942, Marshal Stalin informed General Anders that outbreak of the war in the Pacific had interfered with promised wheat deliveries and

19. See Article 4 of the Treaty.
20. For text, see *Polish-Soviet Relations, 1918-1943, Official Documents,* Issued by Authority of the Government of the Republic of Poland, pp. 126-128.

that therefore the Soviet Government could, from April 1, supply food for only 44,000 of the more than 70,000 Poles then recruited in the Army, none of whom was in active service. In accordance with the desire of the Polish Government, the evacuation to Iran of Polish troops in excess of the 44,000 for whom rations could be supplied was permitted. On June 10, further formation of Polish units in the U.S.S.R. was forbidden and in August, 1942, the remaining 44,000 were evacuated. These Polish divisions have since fought in Africa, Italy and on the western European front, and have assisted in the occupation of Germany.

There were also difficulties about the supervision of relief work and medical help for Poles who had been interned from August to November of 1941 and then released. Polish administration of this work in the U.S.S.R. was liquidated in January, 1943; all Polish institutions, including schools and hospitals, were transferred to the Soviet authorities and later to the care of the Union of Polish Patriots in the U.S.S.R. This was done because the Russians felt that local Polish groups charged with this administration, were in reality spying on the U.S.S.R. Official Polish sources referred vaguely to these difficulties in their statement that "substantial differences developed between the Polish and the Soviet Governments in the winter of 1942 to 1943."

A new calamity was the disappearance of thousands of Polish officers who had been prisoners of war of Russia. As early as January, 1942, following less formal inquiries, the Polish Minister for Foreign Affairs delivered a note to M. Bogomolov, Soviet Ambassador, calling the latter's attention to the fact that a considerable number of Polish army officers, prisoners of war, had not as yet been released or located. The Soviet answer was that all officers had been set free. This circumstance naturally was no secret to Germany who used it for her own ends. In April, 1943, German radio and press announced the discovery of a mass cemetery of Polish army officers in the forest of Katyn, near Smolensk, then under German occupation.

The Polish Government appealed to the International Red Cross to make an investigation and establish the facts on the spot. This act the Soviet Union apparently considered the last straw, and on April 25, 1943, replied with a note which broke off diplomatic relations with the Polish Government.

Poland's action concerning the officers was called by M. Malinowski,[21] formerly a member of the Polish Underground Labor Movement and a follower of the Government-in-exile, "the unfortunate step taken by the Polish Government in addressing the International Red Cross in Geneva." Government circles later made the official explanation that the appeal to

21. See his article "Toward Polish-Soviet Understanding," *New Europe, Supplement,* November, 1943.

the Red Cross was made because no confidence could be placed in German political propaganda.[22] The statement said further:

> On April 16, 1943, the Soviet official news agency TASS published a communiqué concerning the disappearance of the Polish army officers. The Polish Government had waited in vain for more than eighteen months for such a communiqué. According to this statement the Polish prisoners of war who had been doing construction work west of Smolensk, were captured by the Germans during the Soviet retreat in the summer of 1941. The assumption was that they had been murdered by the Germans.
>
> Had this explanation of the capture of the Polish officers by the Germans near Smolensk been given to the Polish authorities at any time during the many conversations and diplomatic exchanges in 1941 and 1943, Poland's appeal to the International Red Cross would not have been made.

In any event, whatever the reasons, the appeal had been made to the Red Cross and the matter led almost immediately to the rupture of diplomatic relations between Poland and the Soviet Union. Following this incident, Poland and Russia became further estranged and, despite the attempts of the Polish Government, first under Sikorski and then—in August, 1943, and later—under Mikolajczyk, to reach a compromise with the U.S.S.R., the deadlock continued. The Polish Government proposed that the United States and Great Britain mediate, but neither party to the dispute altered its viewpoint. However, even if a new pact had been concluded, it could only have ended in further changes. The Russian forces continued their successful offensive against the German Army, which was begun in the spring of 1944, and eventually got beyond the area of the Curzon Line claimed by Moscow, and into Poland itself, thereby creating an entirely new situation. However, before these military developments, Poland's proposal that the United States and Great Britain mediate was based on the assumption that, in both countries, but especially in England, opinion seemed to favor the defense of Poland's territorial *status quo*.

The Polish Government was eager to get in touch with the Soviet Union; although diplomatic relations had been broken off, notes were exchanged in January, 1944, by the Polish and the Soviet Governments (see Appendices). On January 11, 1944, the Soviet Government made Poland the following proposals concerning her borders:

> The Soviet Government does not consider the frontiers of the year 1939 to be unchangeable. The borders can be corrected in favor of Po-

22. *Polish Facts and Figures,* No. 2, March 25, 1944, pp. 21, 22.

land on such lines that districts in which the Polish population predominates be handed over to Poland. In such cases the Soviet-Polish border could approximately follow the so-called Curzon Line, which was adopted in the year 1919 by the Supreme Council of Allied Powers and which provided for the incorporation of the Western Ukraine and Western White Russia into the Soviet Union.

This text hints that the Curzon Line might be corrected for districts where Poles are in the majority, as for instance, in and around Lwow. In the beginning the Polish Government was categorically against the Soviet proposal concerning the Curzon Line. On January 26, 1944, Foreign Secretary Anthony Eden reiterated Prime Minister Churchill's previous statements and reaffirmed the British policy of not recognizing any territorial changes made in Poland since August, 1939 (see Appendices). The Polish Government responded on January 15, 1944, but made no direct answer to the question of the Curzon Line. The emphasis was laid upon unilateral decisions and upon the government's intention to ask for the mediation of the British and American Governments. This constituted a proposal, delicately phrased, to enter into further negotiations concerning the border question. Soviet Russia's statement, which followed on January 17, called Poland's answer a rejection of the Curzon Line.

But as a result of Anglo-American intervention and of the notes sent by Churchill to Stalin, the Polish Government began to move closer to the Russian viewpoint. In the second half of February, 1944, Underground forces were instructed to give "unequivocal co-operation" to the Red Army commanders. On the question of borders, the Polish Government proposed that a temporary demarcation line for administrative purposes be established somewhere between the Curzon Line and the 1939 Russo-Polish boundary. The Poles were to administer the areas west of this line liberated by the Red Army. After the war, and following elections held in Poland, a new government would negotiate for permanent boundaries, expecting as compensation for Eastern losses certain sections of Germany and East Prussia. This proposal too was rejected by the Soviet Union.

But as the successful Soviet forces advanced into the eastern districts of pre-war Poland in the first days of April, 1944, some military co-operation took place between the Polish Underground and the Soviet armies. Orders of co-operation given to the Underground in 1944 by their Government repeated the instructions of January 5, 1944, and of October 27, 1943, to avoid all conflicts with Soviet armies entering Poland. These last orders were given in April despite the fact that the Soviet Government ignored a Polish proposal to co-operate with Soviet commanders "in the event of resumption of Polish-Soviet relations." At this time the Polish Telegraph Agency published instructions to Underground leaders concerning their behavior toward Soviet commandos. These instructions read in part:

Acting under orders from the Polish government delegates in Poland, we meet the forces of the Soviet Union on Polish soil as co-fighters against our common enemy, Germany. We inform you that there exists in these territories an administration secretly organized by the Polish state under the yoke of German occupation.

Unfortunately the first of these orders had, in October, 1943, been interpreted as referring to General Sosnkowski's administration of the occupied and liberated areas. According to this interpretation, the Soviet authorities would have been indirectly recognizing Poland's right to her territory as indicated by the border settlement of 1921. But as the Soviet army advanced beyond these borders they reached territory which the Soviet claimed as both historically and ethnographically Russian, being east of the line drawn when Germany invaded Poland and the Russians moved in from the East. The Soviet commanders were hardly likely to welcome such statements as those above, but they were now on Polish soil and should in theory turn over authority to the Poles by the sovereign right of their government. We cannot here go into details concerning the relations between the advancing Soviet army and the local Polish Undergrounds, beyond stating that this sector was the only one which offered any prospect of ending the deadlock in Polish-Russian relations.

Serious modifications in these relations followed a new crisis in the National Council and in the Government initiated by the Polish Leftist Socialists and the Peasant Laborites. According to the Polish press these changes had no connection with the invitation to visit Moscow, extended by Russia to the American-Polish priest Orlemanski, and to Professor Lange. With the Government-in-exile and the National Council as its parliament, working on the basis of the Polish Constitution of 1935, which had been semi-Fascist and was now an anachronism; and with two of the most important political posts, the State President and the Commander-in-Chief and successor to the President held respectively by Raczkiewicz and General Sosnkowski, both members of the OZON group, which belonged neither to the Cabinet nor to the National Council, a deadlock was inevitable among these various political factions.

The opposition was preparing steps which were taken about the middle of May, 1944. At this time the Socialist members of the Council began to campaign to wrest control from the Rightist military group, to put it in the hands of the civil government, and in general to make the Polish Government more democratic. The Council unanimously agreed to ask President Raczkiewicz to remove the Commander-in-Chief, General Sosnkowski, from his political office as successor to the President, though not from his post as Military Commander. A second motion of the Council demanded the resignation of Lieutenant General Kukiel as Minister of National Defense because of the manner in which he had handled charges of anti-semitism in the Polish armed forces. A third and very important motion called for the creation of a defense committee with both military and civilian members, but this vote was postponed until after certain necessary changes had been made in matters of organization.

Although Polish circles in London asserted that these proposals had no connection with an effort to reach an understanding with the Soviet Union, there is actually no doubt that such was the real motive behind them.

3. The Ukraine

THE ATTITUDE of the Ukrainians concerning the question of the south-eastern frontier of pre-1939 Poland is a result of both national consciousness and history. As they constitute a majority of the population in that area, the Ukrainians form an ethnographic continuation of the Ukraine itself. There is therefore a strong argument for reuniting those districts in which the majority are Ukrainians with the main body of the Ukrainian people, or at least so arranging it that they no longer belong to the Polish commonwealth.

It was stated in the introductory chapter that the Ukraine has a much deeper political and historical background than has White Russia. While the latter occupied a relatively small area, of about 90,000 square miles, the lands inhabited by the Ukrainians in Russia alone cover 200,000, not including Carpatho-Ruthenia which was a part of Czechoslovakia from 1919 to 1939, and Bukovina, a part of Rumania during the same period. In the period after the first World War the Ukrainians in the U.S.S.R., Poland, Rumania, Czechoslovakia and Hungary occupied approximately the same areas which they occupied centuries ago.[1]

Modern Ukrainian nationalism dates from about the middle of the nineteenth century. In Austria, or more accurately Eastern Galicia, self-determination for the Ukrainians developed more strongly, even under Polish political predominance, than in Czarist Russia where all Ukrainian literature, including the translation of the Bible, was prohibited; and for this reason Austrian Galicia was the Piedmont of Russian Ukrainians in the second half of the nineteenth century.

After the February 1917, or Kerensky, revolution in Russia, a far-reaching autonomy was granted the Ukraine, which, after the Bolshevist upheaval in November 1917, was transformed into political independence and the Ukrainian Republic emerged. Since then the Ukraine has undergone a process of frequent political changes. The German-Austrian mili-

1. According to official Soviet data, as of July 1, 1941, the Ukrainian Soviet Republic had a population of more than forty-two millions of which 80 per cent were Ukrainians, 9 per cent Russians, and more than 5 per cent Jews. (See *Soviet Russia Today,* July, 1944, pp. 26-27.) In the United States and Canada the Ukrainian population is estimated at approximately 1,500,000.

tary occupation of the whole of the Russian Ukraine lasted from March, 1918, until the general defeat of the Central Powers in the late fall of that year. The German authorities replaced a moderate Ukrainian democracy by a special, officially pro-Ukrainian, puppet regime headed by General Skoropadski, formerly in the royal guard of the Czar, a Ukrainian of Russian descent. There was a return of democracy for a brief period after the evacuation of the Germans. In January, 1919, the East Galician Ukrainian Republic proclaimed its union with the Ukrainian Republic proper, led by the Russian Ukrainian Petlura, and this united Ukraine entered upon a joint campaign against the Poles in East Galicia and the invading Red armies in the Ukraine.

The clashes and encounters between the Ukrainians and the Poles continued during the sessions of the Supreme Council of the Peace Conference.[2] On June 25, 1919, the Supreme Council authorized a Polish military occupation of Eastern Galicia and simultaneously informed the Ukrainian population that a form of plebiscite would be granted them in order to decide to whom Eastern Galicia belonged. A provisional Polish civil government was introduced, and later the promised plebiscite was withdrawn. Finally, on March 15, 1923, the Conference of Ambassadors assigned Eastern Galicia to Poland, with the understanding "that a regime of autonomy is necessitated by ethnographic conditions." Poland never complied with this moral obligation laid upon her.[3] On the contrary, Ukrainian self-determination was looked upon askance despite a minority treaty signed by Poland at Versailles on June 28, 1919. Instruction in the Ukrainian language was also restricted by decrees of 1924-25 which introduced bilingual schools in the place of those that were purely Ukrainian. Compulsory colonization of Polish soldiers and civilians in frontier districts, and the "pacification" of 1930[4] were the basic trends of post-war Poland's attitude toward her Ukrainian population.

As a result of these prolonged and complicated developments, Ukrainian nationalism increased rapidly in Poland, embracing not only the intelligentsia and the urban middle classes, but the Ukrainian peasantry as well.

The most moderate political movement was that led by the U.N.D.O., that is, the Ukrainian National Democratic Party. This party was represented in the Parliament, or Seym, and even in the Upper House, or the Polish Senate. An agreement was reached, at the end of 1935, between the U.N.D.O. and the Polish government; but after December, 1938, following

2. On May 22, 1919, the vice President of the Ukrainian delegation, Paneyko, protested in a letter to Clemenceau against the extension of the Polish frontiers to the east of what was later called the Curzon Line, and asked for the establishment of ethnographical frontiers. Cf. David Hunter Miller, *My Diary*, Vol. X, p. 322, ff., Vol. XVIII, pp. 468-488.

3. See Chapter II, "Poland: Its Approach to the Issue."

4. See Chapter V.

the rejection by the Seym of very moderate autonomy for the Ukrainians, relations between them became mutually hostile.

The non-parliamentary O.U.N., or Organization of Ukrainian Nationalists, was radical, terrorist, nationalistic. This group sabotaged the "pacification" movement by extremely violent acts, even to burning of the houses of Polish colonists. It was connected with a secret body, the U.M.O., or Ukrainian Military Organization, established in Berlin and led by a former Austrian officer, Konovalec, who was assassinated in 1938. Konovalec was also connected with the illegal anti-Communist Ukrainian nationalist movement in the Soviet Ukraine, about 1933 or 1934.

It might be said that in 1944 the demand for the reunion of all areas populated by Ukrainians was the common denominator of all Ukrainian factions. This was true also of Ukrainian Americans, if the organs of their press in America may be taken as representative of their wishes. Aside from this demand, a number of other tendencies were to be noted among them. Circles grouped around the bi-weekly *Svoboda*, or *Freedom*, represented the anti-Soviet Rightists. This faction was much more vociferous before the second World War. Its most extreme wing was affiliated with the Hitlerite policy in Germany. In the years preceding the war the Nazis used the Ukrainian emigrants' resentment of the Soviet Union's absorption of an independent Ukraine to develop a vehement propaganda for the restoration of the Ukrainian State. General Skoropadski, who was for a short time "Hetman" or Head of the independent Ukraine, supported by the Imperial German occupational forces from 1918 to 1920, emigrated to Germany and remained there for the inter-war period as a friend of the pan-German militarists. When the war began, however, although Skoropadski was obviously a confirmed anti-Soviet, his friendliness with the Prussian military opposition prevented his being actively used as a Nazi Quisling or as an important figure in the Ukraine under Nazi occupation.

The 1941-1944 Nazi occupation, accompanied by terror and starvation imposed upon the Slavic "inferior" population of the Soviet Ukraine, was unable to evoke anti-Russian sentiment such as was produced by the occupation of the Ukraine by Imperial Germany in 1918. On the contrary there is good reason for the assertion that the loyalty of the Ukrainian population to the Soviets increased during the occupation by the Germans; and this includes also the peasantry which, following almost ten years of Soviet collectivization, underwent three years of organized, compulsory economic regimentation and exploitation by a Nazi agricultural authority that exercised a radical control of all production, from the gathering of harvests to the supply and consumption of every egg.

The Ukrainian peasantry, having lived under better economic circumstances than the Russian peasantry, were more concerned with private ownership and therefore suffered more than the White Russians when collective farms were established in the Soviet Union.[5] A considerable number of American Ukrainians stem from these rural classes and so remain to various degrees opposed to the Soviet regime. But Allied victories over Germany, though won by the Soviets, and the consequent liberation of Ukrainian soil from the retreating Germans brought about a kindlier feeling towards the Soviets even in these circles. Memories of the German occupation of 1918-1920—to say nothing about the recent, more devastating Nazi occupation—memories of requisitioning, of pillage and destruction, and of the arbitrary conduct of the military and civil administration, combined with a deeply-rooted hatred of the Germans, gave even these anti-Soviet Ukrainians an incentive to compromise.

Svoboda, however, expressed apprehension from time to time lest the Kremlin's promises of post-war liberation of the Ukraine were not honestly meant. On the twenty-fifth anniversary of Lithuania's sovereignty, in its issue of February 25, 1943, *Svoboda* expressed the fear that, just as the promised liberation of the Vilna district and its inclusion in Lithuania was turned into an aggrandizement of the Soviet Union, when, in June, 1940, the Soviets annexed both the Vilna district and Lithuania, so the liberation of the Ukraine might suffer a similar fate.

In February, 1943, this question came to a head when Alexander Korneitchuk, member of the Supreme Soviet of the Ukrainian Soviet Republic, in an article published in the *Soviet Ukraine,* and later reprinted in *Pravda,* called for a refusal of all demands of the Poles, and demanded that the White Russian and the Ukrainian areas, which had formerly been Eastern Polish territory, should be retained by Russia. The article was actually directed against certain Polish politicians and publicists in London, in particular against Bielecki and others connected with the Polish Government-in-exile. Korneitchuk called them "landlord imperialists" who were opposing the union of the Ukrainian people in order to protect their own narrow social interests in the Western Ukraine where, before the war, 88 per cent of the land belonged to the Polish nobility of whom they are members.

The American Ukrainian paper *Svoboda* supported Korneitchuk's claims against Poland but took pains not to be identified with Ukrainian Bolshevism in general, as may be seen in the issue of February 24, 1943. In *Svoboda's* issues of February 18 and 19 Professor M. Chubaty clearly described the attitude of the Rightist circles. His desire is to see the Ukraine free from both German and Russian domination. He cites the common

5. Some eastern Galicia Ukrainian peasants were, under Soviet occupation in 1939-1941, deported to Siberia together with some groups of Ukrainian "national-revolutionary" intelligentsia.

political and historical background of all Ukrainians, who, he says, ever since the days of the Ukrainian King Danilo, in 1250, have demonstrated their political maturity and their capacity for statesmanship. Professor Chubaty also points out that in their recent past, on January 22, 1919, the Western Ukrainians joined the great Eastern group to form one United Ukrainian Republic. He repudiates the outcome of the October, 1939, plebiscite which was favorable to the absorption of the Western Ukraine into the Soviet Union. "Anyone," he says, "who knows the attitude of the Ukrainian majority and of the Polish and Jewish minorities toward Russian Communism, knows also that under free voting conditions not more than 10 per cent would have favored absorption." He asks for an independent Western Ukraine which "should have the right to join freely in a kind of federation with the independent democratic neighbor states. In any event, the people themselves should decide their future." While admitting that the Western Ukraine is only a part of the whole Ukraine, this is Professor Chubaty's interpretation of the Atlantic Charter for Western Ukrainians.

In January, 1943, a congress of Americans of Ukrainian extraction was convoked by the Rightists in Philadelphia. It was attended by representatives of Rightist organizations, of *Svoboda,* and by many politically nonpartisan or wholly indifferent Ukrainian Americans. The extreme Rightists, adherents of the Hetman regime, also sent delegates. The most important resolution, introduced by Professor Chubaty, demanded an independent Western Ukraine but it was definitely rejected. The congress as a whole, however, was somewhat hostile to any idea of unifying all Ukrainians under the Soviet Union.

The central democratic wing of Ukrainian Americans took still another attitude. Here the opinion prevailed that the destiny of the Ukraine should be determined not by outside forces but by the inhabitants themselves. In an article in the New York *Gromadski Golos*[6] of February 1, 1944, Miroslav Sichinsky stated that there need be no distrust of the U.S.S.R.; that although the Soviet Government would not swing toward an American or British brand of liberalism after the war, yet, in order to retain American and British friendship, it would have to make many changes in policy.

Also, the Ukrainian people manifest a greater degree of national consciousness than before the war, and while this has not yet developed to a point necessary for complete independence, there is every indication that the Ukraine will not permit itself to be culturally submerged and that it will play an important role, in both economics and politics which will surely manifest itself in a movement for greater independence. Partly this found

6. *Gromadski Golos,* the organ of democratic opinion among Ukrainian immigrants in America.

its expression in the granting to the Ukraine of a separate vote at the San Francisco Conference.

Gromadski Golos of March 1, 1944, carried an article devoted to the discussion of Prime Minister Churchill's statement in Parliament that Britain had never guaranteed the precise Eastern boundaries of Poland or the inclusion of Vilna, and emphasized the fact that the Eastern boundaries of Poland are a question not simply of political strategy and political security but primarily of ethnographic frontiers between territories populated by Ukrainians and by Poles. For the Ukrainians to recognize the Curzon Line is but to follow a natural law. This law would include the right of Western Ukrainians to self-determination and to union with the main body politic of the Ukraine. For centuries there has been in the Western Ukraine a longing to unite with Kiev, a trend which reached its peak, throughout all the Ukraine, after the recent struggle against German occupation. To the Ukrainian people, "historical" Poland has always represented a national threat. The only hope of peaceful co-operation between a united Ukraine and its Polish and Russian neighbors lies in the establishment of an "all Ukraine" along the lines indicated above.

Certain other groups which, until the outbreak of the second World War, generally opposed the Soviet regime and its economic and political measures in the Soviet Ukraine after its absorption in 1920, belonged to the Central Democratic Wing of Ukrainians. They now vehemently oppose the claims of Poland regarding the old Riga border line. They reject all Rightist attempts to secure Western Ukrainian independence. But being made up mostly of former Ukrainian Socialist Revolutionaries and of Social Democrats who since 1904 and 1905 have joined in the liberation movement of Russia, these groups look with skepticism and mistrust upon the political policy which might be followed by the Communist Party in a Sovietized Western Ukraine.

A third viewpoint was clearly stated in an article by N. Grigorjev in the *Ukrainski Golos,*[7] or *The Voice of the Ukraine,* of February 2, 1944. The author charged both the U.S.S.R. Leftists and the Polish Rightists with the same imperialist and reactionary character. He regarded the 1921 Riga peace treaty as an attack upon Ukrainian statehood and as a violation of it, being simply a division of the territory between two conquerors. And in the second World War, even before the common enemy, Germany, had been beaten, Poland and the Soviet Union were already fighting each other like two slave-owners, for the future possession of the Ukrainian slaves. Grigorjev went on to ask that the third element of the struggle, the Ukrainian people themselves, be taken into consideration and accorded their legal

7. *Ukrainski Golos,* bi-weekly, Winnipeg, Canada.

place. The Russian-Polish Ukrainian quarrel, he said, could be settled only on the basis of equal rights for all three nations.

Among the Ukrainian emigrés, and among the intelligentsia and peasantry of the Eastern and particularly of the Western Ukraine itself, the idea of Ukrainian sovereign statehood independent of both Soviet Russia and Poland, has been a political ideal of the radical nationalists. Such aspirations have been nurtured by the fear of growing friendly relations between the new Poland and the Soviet Union. For the Ukrainians there appeared to be a certain threat to the realization of an independent Ukraine in this peaceful accord. Some ground for this apprehension might have been found in the persistent rumor that the non-aggression pact of 1932 between Poland and Russia contained secret clauses stipulating that "both governments would follow parallel policies directed against Ukrainian nationalism in their respective countries."[8]

Nevertheless, the sovietization of the eastern Ukraine since the beginning of the 1920's, now deeply rooted in the psychology of the Ukrainian population, and especially the events of the war during which Russia's paramount role in fighting the German menace became obvious once again to almost the entire population of the Eastern and Western Ukraine, have minimized to a great extent any separatist movements directed toward an independent Ukraine of the type dreamed of by the radical nationalists.

8. Buell, R. L., *Poland: Key to Europe* (London, 1939) p. 278; Paneyko, B., "Autour du problème Ukrainien," *L'Esprit International*, Janvier, 1939.

4. White Russia

THE TERRITORY inhabited by the White Russians, that in which about 90 per cent of the farming population are White Russians, lies along the northern part of Eastern Poland. Its inhabitants are, for the most part, poor and often landless peasantry, a fact which has a bearing upon their favorable attitude towards the collective farming initiated by the Soviet Union after 1930. Their cultural history is naturally very scant. Some steps were made after the beginning of the nineteenth century to develop a local literature free from Polish influence. Books began to appear, for the first time, in the White Russian language, one of them being a translation of the *Aeneid*. After the Polish insurrection against Russia in 1863, however, the Russian Government suppressed not only all Polish literature but that of the White Russians as well because they were employing the Polish alphabet in the printing of their books. It was not until after the revolution of 1905 that another period of development of White Russian literature began, and simultaneously there was a new movement toward autonomy.

White Russia was nominally independent for only a short time after the first World War. When the territory was freed from German occupation, in December, 1918, the movement for White Russian independence developed to such a point that a delegation purporting to represent Democratic White Russia was sent to the Paris Peace Conference. As early as January, 1919, a special manifesto of the revolutionary Soviet Government declared that White Russia was "independent," belonging to the Soviet Republics of Russia.[1] Even at the Peace Conference the political movement of the White Russians showed the divided opinions of a border people. There was a recognition of the fact that it was premature to talk of a White Russian state with full independence, because the White Russians themselves inclined toward federation with their neighbors, either with the Poles, the Lithuanians, or the Russians, as the case might be.

First, there was a request for an alliance with Poland, made by "The White Ruthenian Territorial Congress," and transmitted to the Paris Peace

1. *The Policy of Soviet Power Concerning the Nationalities Problem* (Russian, Moscow, 1920), pp. 23-25; Gorbunov, "Lenin and Stalin in their Struggle for the Independence of the White Russian People," *The Historical Journal* (Russian, 1944, No. 2-3).

Conference by the Polish delegation in May, 1919.[2] This Congress was an illegal body which met in the last week of January, 1919, when White Russia was under Bolshevik occupation. It is impossible to evaluate the extent to which the Congress was representative of White Russia, as such, but its pro-Polish tendency was clearly shown by its statement that the existence of an independent White Russian State was impossible and that therefore it should be absorbed by Poland. Nevertheless, the statement went on to outline the conditions under which this annexation should take place, namely, "that within its ethnographical limits, White Ruthenia shall be closely bound to the Polish Republic for the purpose of guaranteeing it economic and cultural development, while at the same time preserving a White Ruthenian national constitution."[3] This declaration was signed by Zwirko-Goditsky, president of the National Territorial Council of White Ruthenia (Bialarusskaya Kraievaya Narodnaya Rada).

At the same time another wing of the White Russian movement developed a more intransigent approach toward complete independence; this was expressed in a protest which was sent to the Paris Peace Conference, May 8, 1919, signed by the "Democratic Republic of White Ruthenia." This self-styled government was established after the withdrawal of the Germans, in December, 1918. It protested against the movement of the Polish troops who came in to White Russia as the Germans withdrew, pointing out that the Polish troops had established themselves in the government of Grodno and occupied "Vilna, the former capital of the White Ruthenian-Lithuanian State from which the inhabitants themselves had already driven out the Bolshevists."[4] In other words, "the Democratic Republic of White Russia" was equally opposed to Bolsheviks and Poles.

As far back as December, 1918, a Bolshevist Moscow, with the active participation of Stalin himself, decided to create a White Russian Soviet Republic, but the project could not be carried out in the atmosphere of the Russian civil war and the Polish invasion of White Russia, which at the beginning was very sucessful. In August, 1919, the Red Army was beaten by the Polish Army which captured the capital, Minsk. Soviet White Russia was finally established only after the liberation of the White Russian territory in August, 1920. It was in this hectic, transitional period prior to August, 1920 when the ephemeral White Russian bourgeois state tried to

2. David Hunter Miller's *Diary*, Volume XVIII, contains the files of the Bulletin of the American Commission to Negotiate Peace, as a continuation and completion of these bulletins commented on in Volume XVII. The files were collected by Miller. Bulletin No. 270 (May 14, 1919) contains: (i) *White Ruthenian Request for Annexation to Poland*, transmitted by the Polish Delegation, (ii) *Telegram from the Walloons and Dinant*, Belgium.

3. *Op. cit.*, XVIII, 230-232.

4. *Ibid.*, XVIII, 381-385. Efforts were made to form a joint Lithuanian and White Russian Republic.

establish a kind of political independence. But with the victory of Poland over the U.S.S.R. the White Russian Government disappeared, and White Russia was divided by the Treaty of Riga, in 1921, between Poland and Soviet Russia. On December 30, 1922, together with the Russian Federative Soviet Republic, the Ukrainian Soviet Republic, and the Transcaucasian Federative Soviet Republic, Soviet White Russia became one of the four "founding" states of the Great Soviet Federation.

There is no doubt that, in the years which followed, the improvement in literacy of Soviet White Russia, the development in science and in a national art and music, of its folklore and of its press, influenced the White Russians of Poland—deprived of any such traces of national cultural autonomy—and inclined them toward union with Soviet Russia.

Unlike the Poles and the Ukrainians, the White Russians have no press organs of their own in the United States and Canada, and therefore in public opinion their emigrés have found no expression. The Ukrainian-American press did, from time to time, mention the White Russian issue but always as though it were identical with the Ukrainian. As for the White Russians in Soviet Russia proper, their approach to the problem of the Curzon Line and to related territorial and political issues coincides with the Soviet attitude.

Moreover, it is to be noted that for almost a quarter century of the Soviet regime in White Russia the country underwent a process of peaceful industrial and cultural development. As compared with the year 1913, the industrial production of this Union Republic increased twenty-three fold; the production of electric power was 110 times greater, and 9720 tractors, representing 349,000 horse power, worked the fields of the Kolkhozes. Other agricultural machines, in tens of thousands, aided the work of the peasantry in what, throughout the years of Czarism, was agriculturally one of the most backward regions of Russia. Approximately two million children received regular instruction in thirteen thousand public schools, both elementary and secondary. There were twenty-six institutions of higher learning, including universities, in Soviet White Russia, and 95 technical schools of a secondary type.[5] In contrast, a majority of the population of the western part of White Russia, under Polish domination from 1919-20 to 1939, were far from being contented—socially, politically, or culturally. For them conditions in Soviet White Russia were ideal.

While it is impossible accurately to measure public opinion in an area like that inhabited by the White Russians as a whole, it has been pointed out above that the farming population of that part of it lying within the Soviet Union—and it is the greater part—has shown a loyal attitude toward the Union. There was no way for the White Russians who remained under

5. *Bielaruss* (White Russian bi-Monthly, No. 1, 1944).

German occupation of showing their pro-Soviet orientation. But the German occupational authorities were eager to demonstrate them as opposed to the Soviet Union and favoring German rule. That is perhaps why, under German occupation, a pro-German White Russian National Council was established in Minsk, the capital, with the function of a restricted puppet representative of White Russian public opinion. On March 10, 1944, this Council went so far as to order general mobilization of a White Russian Army to "protect" the country against a friendly, liberating army of the Soviet Union.

The war for the "fatherland," since 1941, has undoubtedly strengthened White Russian sentiment for the Soviet Union. Indicative of this is a proclamation, published in *Izvestia*, on August 8, 1943, from White Russian fighting men to the entire White Russian people and to their partisans. It reads in part:

> For thee, O White Russia, in this war for the fatherland, White Russians are fighting in the ranks of the Red Army at the front: one hundred and eight generals, hundreds of colonels and hundreds of thousands of warriors. Thy sons are fulfilling with devotion the traditional claim of our fathers and ancestors to a union of blood with the Russian and Ukrainian people. As the great river Dnieper is powerful and united— the Dnieper which nourished the ancient tribes of Russians, White Russians and Ukrainians—so, too, are united our history, our culture, our aspirations and our interests.

5. The Soviet Union

THE MOST COMPLETE statement of the official Soviet approach to Poland and its present problems was made by the Moscow bi-weekly, *The War and the Working Class,* in an article published on January 15, 1944, entitled "Poland, Our Neighbor," and signed by N. Baltiski, obviously a pseudonym.

Disregarding all acts of the Czarist Government which had favored an independent Poland, as well as the declaration of the Kerensky Government upon which the victorious nations based their recognition of Poland in 1919,[1] *The War and the Working Class* declares that the Soviet Revolution in Russia played the most important part in the restoration of Poland's independence. The truth of the matter, however, is that in this respect Soviet Russia simply followed the steps of its predecessors. As early as November, 1917, the Soviet Government had asserted the right of all the peoples of Russia to self-determination and officially admitted the inalienable right of the Polish people to independence and unity. On August 29, 1918, all the treaties of the Czarist regime concerning the partition of Poland were declared null and void. This article goes on to say:

> The declaration of 1917 laid the cornerstone for the rebirth of independent Polish statehood. At the time, the Polish state did not yet exist and Poland was occupied by the German Army. After Germany's defeat in November, 1918, the "Council of Regents" appointed by German occupational authorities ceded its power to Pilsudski who had led the Polish legions of the Austro-German army in the war. Instead of demanding a real restoration of Poland, Pilsudski and his followers were completely satisfied by a kind of German protectorate over the Polish districts (gubernias), formerly under Imperial Russia. The Ukrainian and White Russian territories, intended to be subordinated to Germany, were not even mentioned, while Poznan and Western Galicia, with

1. See preamble to the Treaty with Poland signed at Versailles on June 28, 1919: "Whereas by the proclamation of March 30, 1917, the Government of Russia assented to the establishment of an independent Polish State. . . ." The Treaty intentionally prefers to quote the recognition of Poland by the Russian Democratic Government rather than that by the Soviet Government.

Cracow, were to remain in the hands of Germany and Austro-Hungary. It was not until after German imperialism had fallen that Pilsudski forgot the former modesty of his demands and began to hunger for territories belonging to other states.

After Poland was recognized, at Versailles, as an independent state Pilsudski tried to realize his old dream by incorporating the whole Soviet Ukraine to the west of the river Dnieper down to Odessa, as well as Soviet White Russia, in the new State.

The Poles began war against the Soviets in the spring of 1920; they invaded Soviet Ukraine and occupied Kiev. A month later they were driven from Kiev by the Soviet armies in a counter-offensive which reached to the suburbs of Warsaw. Poland was then ready to modify her aggressive plans and inclined toward a negotiated peace with Russia. Soviet Russia had been weakened by a long war and by economic difficulties and still had to maintain military forces against White Russian counter-revolutionaries, so she also, on her side, was compelled to make important concessions to the Polish aggressors. Poland was rejecting the Soviet proposal of a democratic plebiscite of Eastern Galicia, and by the Riga Treaty of 1921 Western Ukraine and Western White Russia remained annexed to Poland. Thus Poland ignored the decision of the Supreme Council in 1919 that the "Curzon Line" should mark the Eastern borderline of Poland and leave Western Ukraine and Western Russia to be incorporated into the Soviet Union.

Here the author goes on to quote almost word for word the Soviet declaration of January 11, 1944. In reality, however, as the Polish Government pointed out, the Curzon Line never constituted a boundary between Poland and the U.S.S.R. The Polish view, based on the Supreme Council's decision at the Spa Conference,—not in 1919, but in 1920—was that the Curzon Line was meant to be only a temporary demarcation "without prejudging the provisions which must in the future define the Eastern frontiers of Poland."[2]

The author of the article continues:

It is no secret that Poland was supported both in the preparation and in the conduct of the war against Soviet Russia by the Entente. After German imperialism was defeated in 1918, these governments began to organize military intervention, in order to overthrow Soviet power and dismember our country. Making a rapid change of masters, Pilsudski and his followers turned from serving German imperialists to serving the French. Who knows if Poland might not have been a peaceful country if

2. Cf. *Polish Facts and Figures*, No. 2 (March 25, 1944, published by the Polish Information Center) p. 6.

the Versailles Treaty had limited her territory to her ethnographical frontiers and had clearly stated: "This is your country. Behave peacefully and your security and independence are guaranteed. But if, on the contrary, you interfere with the security of your neighbors, you will do so on your own responsibility." But the victorious powers said nothing of the kind to the Poles. Instead it was whispered that the mission of the Polish State was to become "a bastion of the West against the East," and to play a dominant role in fighting Soviet Russia and establishing a *cordon sanitaire* along the Russian frontiers. This attitude deprived the Polish lords of their last possible vestiges of good judgment. Poland, being a young country, needed reciprocal trade relations more than the Soviet Union, yet the Polish rulers did not wish to develop any regular commodity exchange or allow the importation of Soviet manganese and iron, and of raw cotton and cotton yarn which before 1914 Poland had imported from Russia in huge quantities. Polish industry needed the Soviet Union as a market even more than Soviet raw materials, yet it was with Germany that Poland maintained her most active economic contact. Her exports to Germany constituted 24 per cent of her entire export, that to England 18.2 per cent, to the United States 5.3 per cent, but to the Soviet Union only 1.01 per cent. Moreover, German capital controlled the key positions of Polish industry, not to mention important investments of French, American, Belgian and British capital. These facts demonstrate the somewhat fictitious character of the economic and political independence of Poland.

The author then discusses at even greater length the attitude of Poland to her Ukrainian and White Russian minority populations:

At the demand of the Soviet Government, a special article, Article 7, was included in the Soviet Peace Treaty, with Poland of March, 1921, granting certain rights of nationality, language and religion to the Russian, Ukrainian and White Russian population of Poland. If the Poles had really desired to establish good neighbor relations with the Soviet Union, they would have observed these rights of their own national minorities and realized that the people of the Soviet Union could not be indifferent to the fate of their "blood brothers" in Western Ukraine and Western White Russia.

A series of international agreements during the first years of Poland's existence bound her to certain obligations concerning her national minorities, Article 93 of the Versailles Treaty bound Poland to grant the national minorities in her territory equal rights with the Poles. A special treaty concerning the protection of minorities was signed by Poland and the Entente powers on June 28, 1919. According to this treaty the national minorities were entitled to enjoy equal political rights with those of the dominant nation, equal rights to appointments for the state civil service, the right to use their own mother tongue in public establishments, etc. Finally, on March 15, 1923, the Supreme Council of the Allied Powers expressed the decision that "Poland recognizes that the ethnographical conditions of Eastern Galicia demand an autonomous regime for this area."[3]

But all these promises remain only on paper and Poland recklessly disregarded her obligations toward her national minorities. Time and again the Soviet Government was compelled to call the attention of the Polish Government to Article 7 of the Riga Treaty. In the Soviet note of May 10, 1924, it was pointed out that: "It is impossible to cite all the cases of violence and ridicule suffered by the national minorities. Most of these passed without leaving a trace in the public opinion of other countries, due to the inaction of the White Russian and Ukrainian peoples. Terror reigned throughout the whole area of White Russia and Eastern Galicia, filling the people of these regions with fear that, instead of diminishing, these acts of violence and repression might become a regular mass movement."

The Polish rulers subjugated the peoples of Western Ukraine and Western White Russia to the worst type of semi-feudal colonial slavery. Ukrainian and White Russian peasants—the basic population of these areas—lived under intolerable pressure from their Polish landlords. They were land-hungry but had to remain bonded to their owners. In Western Ukraine, only 12 to 13 per cent of the land was in the hands of the peasant population, the rest being owned by the gentry or by military colonists of Polish descent. In Western White Russia 67.6 per cent of the land belonged to a group of only 1,027 Polish squires. In these two border provinces the authorities suppressed all free development of national culture and continuously opposed national schools. When the Polish regime was established in 1919, there were 3,662 Ukrainian schools in Western Ukraine; after twenty years there remained only 135.

These lengthy extracts from *The War and the Working Class* by no means exhaust the Soviet attack upon the policies of Poland, but enough has been given to indicate the deep-rooted sense of the Polish Government's ever-present hostility to the Soviet. The article continues to sketch the history of Poland's foreign policy down to the outbreak of the second World War, pointing especially to the actions of Colonel Beck, the Polish Foreign Minister, and his intrigues against the Soviet, both at Geneva and in the

---

3. The lack of accuracy in the terminology of this whole paragraph could not be corrected in the translation of the Russian original.

capitals of Europe, from 1935 to 1938. In March, 1938, when Germany invaded Austria, the rulers of Poland sent their ultimatum to Lithuania and only by the action of the Soviet Government were they kept from undertaking the conquest of Poland's northern neighbor. Then the article goes on to remind the reader of Poland's willingness to share in the dismemberment of Czechoslovakia by seizing the small district of Teschen. At the same time, the Polish Government did not prepare for the defense of the borders of their country against the danger of a German assault, although the Soviet warned them more than once of this danger. On the other hand, the Polish official paper, the *Kurjer Poranny*, expressed complete trust in the sincerity of Germany's friendship for Poland. The Soviet journal then voices this conclusion: "The Polish Government intended to enter the war on the side of Hitlerite Germany; the whole foreign policy since 1934 was directed to this aim. The reason it did not materialize was that Hitler decided to make Poland not his ally but his victim."

This long quotation from *The War and the Working Class* is, it should be remembered, a wartime document, and by no means an objective statement of history. It is, however, an important document for the understanding of the motives underlying Soviet policy. On the other hand, the formal relations between Moscow and Warsaw during the period after the Treaty of Riga to the opening of the second World War were not unfriendly, as the signing of a non-aggression pact would indicate. The complete change in the Soviet Government's attitude towards Poland came only after Germany had overrun all western Poland, including Warsaw, early in September, 1939. Then, while Poland was helpless and defeated by its western neighbor, it was suddenly invaded by its neighbor on the east, which occupied all of eastern Poland up to the Curzon Line and beyond it in the north and south. Moscow sought to justify this action on the ground that the Polish State no longer existed and that "left to herself and without leadership, Poland would become convenient ground for any dangerous and unexpected happenings which may create a menace to the U.S.S.R." Thus the Soviet Government justified its joining in the new partition of Poland on the basis of its own security.[4]

In a radio broadcast, Mr. Molotov emphasized the point that since the Polish State had ceased to exist, Russian treaties with it, including that of non-aggression, had become null and void. This situation continued to exist until Germany attacked Russia in June 1940.

Soviet Russia's entry into the war against Germany did not immediately bring about an alliance with Great Britain. Although it was Britain's hour of greatest peril during which it stood alone against a victorious Germany, such a complete re-alignment took a week or two for the necessary adjust-

4. See Appendix I.

ments. Finally, however, on July 12, 1941, twenty days after the Nazi invasion of Soviet territory, the first Anglo-Russian treaty was signed. It contained no political obligations and made no reference to the Polish problem. It consisted only of two sentences:

1. The two governments mutually undertake to render each other assistance and support of all kinds in the present war against Hitlerite Germany.

2. They further undertake that during this war they will neither negotiate nor conclude an armistice or treaty of peace except by mutual agreement.[5]

Russo-Polish relations were dealt with in direct negotiations between General Wladyslaw Sikorski, Prime Minister of the Polish Government in London, encouraged by Anthony Eden, and the Soviet Ambassador to Great Britain, Ivan Maisky. These negotiations dealt with the treatment of Polish prisoners of war in Russia and with the problem of the Russo-Polish boundary. Finally, on July 30, 1941, an agreement was signed between the Soviet and the Polish representatives. Article 1 of this agreement reads, "The Government of the U.S.S.R. recognizes the Soviet-German treaties of 1939 as to territorial changes in Poland, as having lost their validity."

Although the British Government was not a formal party to this agreement, Anthony Eden, the British Foreign Minister, gave to General Sikorski a note of agreement with it, stated in identical terms: "His Majesty's Government do not recognize any territorial changes in Poland since August, 1939." General Sikorski, however, kept the door open for future negotiations in a reply which stated the Polish case: "The Polish Government have never recognized *any* changes effected in Poland since the outbreak of the present war." (The italics are not in the original.)

The discrepancy between the two notes is more than verbal. Poland was continuing to maintain a legal case for itself and thus interpreting its agreement with Russia as a concession to present emergencies.

The Polish point of view has been so frequently stated and is so well known that it is unnecessary to develop it here. It may, however, be of interest to compare with it the Soviet point of view as expressed in one of the most important publications, *The Soviet Encyclopaedia*. The article "Poland," in Volume 46 of that authoritative reference guide, was released to the press on June 29, 1940, about a year before Germany's attack on Soviet Russia. This highly official article says among other things:

5. Treaty Series No. 15 (1941) (British), London, Cmd. 6304. Replaced by *Treaty of Mutual Assistance Between Great Britain and the Soviet Union*, Ratifications Exchanged July 4, 1942: British Treaty Series (1942), No. 2, Cmd. 6376.

The treaty of friendship of September 28, 1939, between the U.S.S.R. and Germany definitely fixed the frontiers of both interested partners, concerning the territory of the former Polish state. Article II of this treaty states that "both parties recognize as final the limits set in Article I to their mutual state interests." Thus Article II took the ground from under the feet of those who wanted to have others take their chestnuts out of the fire. The pharisaical weeping over the "historical role of Poland," which we hear from English and French imperialists and the renegades of the Second Internationale, are only crocodile tears, for the catastrophic failure of their hopes.

It was a long way from the situation thus indicated in June, 1940, to the Treaty of July 30, 1941, which marked the creation of a new era of Russian-Polish co-operation. This co-operation was continuous, and resulted in the conclusion on August 14, 1941, of a military convention between Poland and Russia. Loans were also made by the Soviet Government to the Polish Government for the support of Polish divisions in Russia and the relief of Polish citizens in Soviet territory. In December, 1941, General Sikorski visited Moscow, and on December 5 the Polish-Russian Declaration of Friendship and Mutual Aid was signed. All the subsequent events down to the rupture of diplomatic relations between Moscow and the Polish Government are described in Chapter II.

After the severing of diplomatic relations with the Polish Government, *Izvestia* commented as follows on the occasion of the tragic death of General Sikorski:

General Sikorsky belonged in the category of those who understood and evaluated rightly the tremendous significance of the struggle being made by the Soviet Union against Hitlerite Germany for the common good of the freedom-loving peoples. Speaking today of his death, we have to say that his desire for the strengthening of the friendly ties between the U.S.S.R. and Poland was nullified by those circles whose policy proved to be pernicious for pre-war Poland. Nevertheless, the Soviet Union, as before, is of the opinion that after the defeat of Hitler in Europe a powerful and independent Poland must exist, namely, on the basis of durable good neighborhood and mutual respect or, if the Polish people will desire it, on the basis of a union of mutual aid against the Germans as the chief enemies of the Soviet Union and Poland.

Throughout the whole period from the days of Sikorski to the visits of Orlemanski and Professor Lange in the second half of May, 1944, the Soviet Union assured Poland that it was in the interest of the Soviet Union that Poland remain a strong state after the war. In the last interview given by

Premier Stalin to Professor Lange his final words were: "Poland is going to play a very important role in Europe."[6]

This assurance is connected with a conception which appears more and more to permeate the political outlook of Soviet Russia. This is a new kind of pan-Slav movement, or rather of a consciousness that in the future political organizations of Europe the Slavonic nation-states have to play an entirely new rôle. This new pan-Slavism has very little in common with the old pan-Slav movement, the center of which was more outside Russia than inside. The roots of pan-Slavism go back to the eighteenth century, and beyond. It began as a romantic and partly mystical movement interwoven with Utopian ideas and expressed by those under the cultural and political yoke of the old anti-Slav regimes in Southeastern and Eastern Europe. In all these, the Russians themselves were rather the passive supporters than the active participants, although the pan-Slav movement reached home at various times and at various places. The active movement was chiefly directed against the Germanization of Slavic populations in east-central Europe and the Turkish rule in the south. The nineteenth century wars of liberation freed the Balkan Slavs and the first World War liberated the more advanced western Slavs, the Poles, Czechs, Slovaks, Croats and Slovenes, by the defeat of imperial Germany and Austria-Hungary. The era of freedom, however, was short. The second World War brought all of these peoples under the domination of Nazi Germany, which emphasized the racial problem by an obligatory state doctrine that the Slavic peoples were inferior to the Germanic. This lesson was forced upon the Ukrainian and White Russian peoples for more than two years by the terrible occupational regime of the Nazis.

A new center for the Slav movement was created in Russia in recent years, a detailed description of which lies outside the scope of this study. Suffice it to say that a special review, *Slavyane,* is now published in Moscow devoted to the political and cultural interests of all Slav peoples. A new political and historical literature has grown up, of books, pamphlets and articles, and special research studies are now appearing daily, dealing with the history and the future of the Slav peoples. This new pan-Slavism includes Poland as an active participant in a new alliance of the Slavic nations. Although the old pan-Slavism did not embrace the Poles because of their ancient hostility to imperial Russia, a hostility which found voice in two revolutionary uprisings and could not be bridged in the past even by the efforts of certain Polish and Russian thinkers, the new pan-Slavism surmounts the religious barrier between orthodox and Catholic Slavs and the regional and cultural animosities which in the past tended to set the western Slavs against the more backward eastern Slavs.

6. *New York Times,* May 22, 1944.

This new pan-Slav movement will undoubtedly become of increasing importance in the political sphere especially since it concerns relations with Germany, the nursery of that pan-Germanism of which Nazism was the greatest, if the most inhuman, expression. The future attitude of the Slavs toward Germany is complicated by the question of German minorities in the Slavic countries. In Czechoslovakia there were some three million Germans, in Poland more than a million, and in Yugoslavia some six hundred thousand. Migration from East Prussia and some parts of Silesia was apparently involved in the proposal made by the Soviet Union on January 11, 1944. This proposal was formulated as follows:

> Poland's western borders must be extended by joining to Poland the age-old Polish lands taken away from Poland by Germany, without which it is impossible to unite the whole of the Polish people within its own state. It would thus acquire a necessary outlet to the sea.

According to press dispatches from London the decision reached at the Moscow and Teheran Conferences went beyond this declaration: instead of a Polish Corridor in post-war Europe, East Prussia—the breeder of wars—should be given to Poland, not simply as compensation for her eastern provinces (which would be ceded to the Soviet Union) but also for geographical reasons.

The repeated assurances in Moscow that Russia is in favor of a powerful Polish state gain added weight from its attitude toward the other Slavic peoples in Europe. An indirect proof of this is the treaty of the Soviet Union with Czechoslovakia concluded on May 8, 1944, the draft of which received approval in Great Britain and in the United States. This treaty placed the Czechoslovak territory liberated by the Russian armies under the authority of the Russian military command with a Czech administration to take over the government when the area no longer remained a fighting zone. This actually happened in the Spring of 1945. Similar arrangements were worked out in the Balkans. Whether this also means a shifting of the internal regimes of the respective countries to approximately the Soviet pattern is a question which falls outside the scope of this study.

Much more difficult to evaluate is the Soviet reaction to the Polish Underground, because in the very nature of the case, so little is known of the relations between the Underground leaders and Polish political factions. In England and the United States, for many months, hopes were nurtured that a compromise could be reached between Moscow and the Polish Government-in-exile. These hopes, however, were destined to be frustrated, and Moscow grew impatient, as indicated by a cable from London to the *New York Times,* May 5, 1944:

When the time comes for the Red Army to enter that part of Poland west of the old Curzon Line, in pursuit of the Germans, the Russians have no intention of consulting the Polish Government in London about civil administration, any more than they have already done in the eastern territory they claim as their own. Furthermore, the Russians will not only attempt to find leaders for the new government from liberated Poland, but they will resist any attempt by Premier Stanislaw Mikolajczyk to transplant his Cabinet of Exiles, as presently constituted, from London to Polish soil.

Subsequent events have shown that this cable gave a truer picture of the Soviet approach than the more optimistic views of those who believed in the possibility of a Soviet-Polish compromise simply by ousting General Sosnkowski and other Polish Ministers hostile to Moscow.

On May 24, a Moscow radio announced that a pro-Russian National Council of Poland had sent representatives, from German-occupied Polish territory, to Moscow, thus suggesting that the Soviet Union might recognize this Council as the legal government of Poland. The announcement stated that the National Council included representatives of political parties and social groups, the character of which might be described as follows:

The oppositional section of the Peasant party, the Polish Socialist party, the Polish Workers, the Committee of National Initiative [a group of non-party democrats belonging to an illegal trade union movement], the Union of Young Fighters [Valki Mlodykh], the groups of writers, co-operators, intellectual workers, artisans; and representatives of military organizations: the People's Guard, the People's Militia, peasant battalions, and a number of representatives of local military formations of the regional army—the army under General Kasimierz Sosnkowski, Polish Commander in Chief in London, and President-designate, and several others.[7]

The announcement concluded:

Representatives of the National Council of Poland arrived in Moscow, first of all to make themselves familiar with the activities of the Union of Polish Patriots in the U.S.S.R., and with the state of the First Polish

7. The absence of the Polish Communists from this list of parties may be explained by the dissolution of the Communist Party of Poland after the occupation of eastern Poland by the Red Army. (See David J. Dallin, in *Russia and Postwar Europe*, Yale University Press, 1943, p. 203.) However, the Polish Workers Party is considered to be the continuation of the Polish Communist Party.

Army, and secondly, to establish contacts with the Allied Governments, including the government of the U.S.S.R.

If what the broadcast recorded by the Soviet monitor asserts is true, namely, that this pro-Soviet Polish National Council was organized in Warsaw as long ago as January 1, 1944—and there is no reason to doubt it— the Soviet Government's adamantine attitude in the exchange of state- ments with the Polish Government-in-exile, from January 5 to January 17, is more readily understandable. But assertions published in the Soviet press up to the beginning of May, stating that although the Soviet Government had no intention of dealing with the Mikolajczyk Government of London, either then or after the liberation of western Poland, neither did it intend to use the Union of Polish Patriots in Moscow as a puppet to establish a Polish government there, no longer bore up after Moscow's recognition of the representatives of the new Polish National Council. Moreover, the ac- tive participation of the Union of Polish Patriots in the creation and strengthening of the new Council was openly demonstrated in Moscow.

6. Soviet-Polish Relations

IN THE SUMMER of 1944 a new phase developed in Soviet-Polish relations, as the victories of the Soviet Army took it westward, over the frontier, to the soil of Poland. Much of what happened at that time is still undisclosed, especially the true relations of the Soviet armies with the Polish Underground. There is evidence that during German occupation the Underground had divided into two groups, one of which viewed with apprehension the advance of the Soviet armies, fearing that they might only be exchanging one foreign master for another, while the other welcomed them as liberators. It was unfortunate that at this time Mikolajczyk's London Cabinet remained cut off from direct diplomatic relations with Moscow; and the breach was widened as it became evident that the Soviet Government was turning definitely to the Polish Union in Moscow, in spite of its previous statements that the Union would not be used as a puppet government.

A diplomatic offensive began shortly after the opening of the military offensive. On June 22 the Supreme Soviet of the U.S.S.R. issued a decree proclaiming that members of the Polish army and their dependents could opt for Polish citizenship. This decree applied to those Poles who had joined the three Polish divisions[1] under the command of General Zygmunt Berling, former chief of staff for General Anders, who had decided to remain in the Soviet Union. These divisions fought alongside the Russian Army, and on reaching Polish territory proper, were transformed into the Polish Army, under the command of General Rola-Zymierski. On June 23, the Union of Polish Patriots formally repudiated the Polish Government-in-exile. Prior to this, there appeared an article in *Wolna Polska (Free Poland)* which stated that "The Union of Polish Patriots recognizes the National Council of Poland as the representative of the nation."

After the Soviet-Polish armies crossed the frontier into Polish territory, an official Soviet statement was issued, on July 25, 1944, which, after asserting that the Soviet Government was intent upon restoring "a strong, democratic, independent Poland," went on to say:[2]

1. For an interesting first-hand description, see Edmund Stevens, *Russia is No Riddle*, Greenberg, New York, 1945, Chapter 19, *The White Eagle Flies Again*.
2. *New York Times*, July 26, 1944.

It [the Soviet Government] has decided to conclude with the Polish Committee of National Liberation an agreement on relations between the Soviet Command and the Polish administration.

The Soviet Government declares that it does not pursue aims of acquiring any part of Polish territory or of a change of social structure in Poland, and that the military operations of the Red Army on the territory of Poland are dictated solely by military necessity and by the striving to render the friendly Polish people aid in its liberation from German occupation.

According to press reports, Great Britain and the United States had received no previous information from the Soviet Government regarding its recognition of the Polish Committee as the authorized representative of Poland. The State Department made no comment at the time. The Polish Committee in its proclamation asserted that the Government-in-exile was illegal because based on the Fascist Polish Constitution of 1935, whereas the Committee's authority was based on the earlier democratic Constitution of 1921. On the other hand, the Polish Government-in-exile reacted strongly, as was to be expected. Its Ambassador to the United States, Jan Ciechanowski, denounced the Polish Committee as "a typical puppet government imposed by Moscow."

Moscow, however, went on to justify the recognition of the Polish Committee and its National Council on the ground that it actually represented the people of occupied Poland, having been drawn from the People's Councils of the provinces, cities and rural districts of that area. Naturally, the London Poles denied that the new Council possessed any representative character, either from a legal or a purely political standpoint, declaring that it was composed of Polish Communists and left-wing non-Communist politicians.

THE EFFORTS OF THE LONDON POLES TO BRING ABOUT A SOVIET-POLISH COMPROMISE

It should be said of the Polish Government-in-Exile that, notwithstanding all difficulties and rivalries, serious attempts were made by it, and particularly by Premier Mikolajczyk, to heal the breach and to work out a Russo-Polish rapprochement. Toward the end of July, 1944, Premier Mikolajczyk left London for Moscow for the purpose of effecting a settlement that would include the Polish Government-in-exile and the rival, so-styled government Committee of Poland, as well as its Soviet sponsors. At first there was hope of a Soviet-Polish accord, especially since Premier Stalin consented to receive Premier Mikolajczyk—undeniably a noteworthy concession in view of the rupture of diplomatic relations between them.

On August 3, Premier Stalin and Commissar Molotoff conferred with Mikolajczyk, Stanislaw Grabski, Speaker of the Polish National Council in London, and Foreign Minister Tadeusz Romer. Marshal Stalin had expressed the desire that "the problems pertaining to the situation in Poland should be decided by the Poles themselves, and that they should be discussed by M. Mikolajczyk with the Polish Committee of National Liberation."[3] At the meeting of the two groups, Mikolajczyk conceded that there were serious faults in the 1935 Constitution; but the meeting resulted in nothing tangible. The basic question, that of the proposed merger of the two Polish bodies, and a purge of Mikolajczyk's Cabinet of its most outspoken anti-Soviet members, was not settled; and therefore the second question, that of territorial boundaries, was not discussed. Premier Mikolajczyk did, however, gain the consent of the Moscow Poles to include him and at least three other members of his London Cabinet in the future united government; and after making the statement that "Warsaw, which is now fighting a hard and terrible fight, would be the best and easiest place to find agreement," both between the Polish groups and between Russia and Poland in general, he left Moscow, August 10th. He announced that he was returning to London to lay before his Cabinet definite proposals for a new Polish Government.

Toward the end of August, Premier Mikolajczyk, in an effort to meet the demands of Moscow, proposed dropping General Sosnkowski by vacating the post of Commander-in-Chief of the Polish forces. As to the question of Poland's eastern border, the Premier was somewhat inclined to accept a compromise based on the Curzon Line, which was the frontier demanded by the Soviet Union.

THE WARSAW UPRISING

Meanwhile, the military situation in and around Warsaw was further complicated by the uprising of the Warsaw patriots led by "General Bor,"[4] which began on August 1. This heroic and desperate attempt of the Polish Underground to free the capital from the invader could succeed only if supported by the Soviet army, already on the eastern bank of the Vistula. Unfortunately the advance of this army was checked before it could make contact with the Polish troops which were closely encircled by German forces in Warsaw. As the struggle dragged on in a house-to-house battle, strong accusations were made by the Poles against the Soviet Union for its failure to relieve the besieged forces. On the other hand, the leading newspapers of the Soviet Union joined the Polish Committee of Liberation in the serious charges that General Bor had initiated the uprising upon the

3. *New York Times*, August 10, 1944.
4. "Bor" was an assumed name, the officer's real name being Tadeusz Komorowski.

orders of the London Government-in-exile for purposes of political prestige and without the approval of the Soviet army authorities.

The truth as to Russia's responsibility may never be wholly known because, in the world of the "Fighting Underground," few documents were kept. The public utterances which we now have to fall back upon are quite inadequate. The main points, however, may be summarized here. The Moscow bi-weekly, *The War and the Working Class,* of April 15, 1944, commenting editorially on letters to the editor, stated that

> The authors of the letters have their suspicions lest this army [the Polish Underground] has other aims than the struggle against Hitler's invasion.

The thinly-veiled animus of this comment would be readily understood by those reading it. It meant that the Soviet authorities regarded the Polish Underground as by no means a friendly ally.

In midsummer, however, the evidence that Moscow was lending encouragement to the Underground army grew greater. On July 30, the Kosciuszko radio station in Moscow, announcing the approach of the Red Armies, sent an appeal to the Poles in Warsaw in the following terms:

> People of Warsaw, to Arms! The whole population should join the Underground army. Attack the Germans! Attack the Germans! Assist the Red Army in crossing the Vistula. Give it information and show it the best fords over the river. More than a million inhabitants ought to become an army of more than a million fighting for liberation and destroying the German invaders.

There were also thirteen other appeals over Moscow's Kosciuszko radio station urging the Poles to rise and fight the Germans.[5] It must be said that, under the circumstances, all such appeals to resistance by the Poles, whether accompanied by direct promises of help or not, were sure to be interpreted as at least indirect promises, because a mighty belligerent like the Soviet Union would not ask for military action by an Underground army without planning to offer material assistance to the insurgents. But from the sources available at present, it is difficult to come to any clear conclusion concerning the kind of help promised, and the time and place at which it was to be delivered. Therefore, strictly speaking, there is no documentary evidence that the Soviets "went back upon their word." We also need further light upon two historical facts. Why did the Soviet army refuse to allow Allied airplanes which were dropping supplies upon Warsaw the right to land on Soviet airfields? More important still: was the Soviet army badly defeated when it attempted the relief of Warsaw? When it reached Praga, the

5. See the Associated Press Report of August 15, and a letter to the *New York Times,* September 10, 1944, signed by Waclaw Lednicki, one of the Polish emigré leaders.

eastern suburb of Warsaw, it established contacts with Bor's army across the Vistula. But this effort at collaboration was apparently insufficient, and was finally broken off.[6] The tragic episode left a burning trail of recriminations. Early in September, Sosnkowski denounced not only the Russians but the British as well for their "indifference" to the plight of Warsaw.[7] This singularly unconsidered charge was later withdrawn.

AGRARIAN REFORM

Meanwhile, into the arena of political and military strife there were introduced matters of a socio-economic nature which further aggravated the rift between the Polish circles in London and the National Liberation Committee in Lublin. Outstanding among these was the proposal of agrarian reforms by the Committee of Liberation, under which large landed estates, or those exceeding 125 acres (about 50 hectares) of cultivated land would be broken up and parcelled out to peasants and farm-workers to be operated privately or co-operatively, but not collectivized according to the Soviet system. This reform, which would go into effect in late December, 1944, would not affect the estates held by the Roman Catholic church.

Anyone familiar with the history of the Polish revolutionary movement, especially since the uprisings of 1831 and 1863 against Czarism, will recall that, due to the complete lack of agrarian reforms, those upheavals became nationalistic mutinies led by aristocrats and some urban elements not primarily interested in the improvement of the poverty-stricken Polish peasantry. True, there were individuals like Czacky and Staszic who, in the first decades of the nineteenth century, desired to extend the struggle for Poland's home rule and independence to include the demands of the Polish peasantry by a division of the great estates of the nobility and the gentry.

Serfdom was abolished as early as 1807, but, in part, the Polish peasants remained bound to labor on the landlords' estates. Reactionary Czarist Governments made some allotments of land to the Polish peasants in order

6. See *The Polish Review*, published in New York by the Polish Information Center, Vol. IV, No. 38, October, 1944: "All three main Polish military headquarters in Warsaw now have Soviet liaison officers who keep the Red Army in Praga closely informed by radio of Underground successes. Polish-Russian contact has now been so well established that the Home Army often directs Soviet artillery fire across the river. Both the Russians and the British, the latter flying from Italy, continue to supply the Home Army from the air with desperately needed arms, ammunition and food."

7. See *New York Times*, August 25, 1944.

There is a note of justification of the Red Army's action in the Review, *New Statesman and Nation* (London, September 2, 1944), which said: "The Red Army, after a march of several hundred miles was not in the best condition to storm the city [Warsaw] across the Vistula. . . . With the Poles holding only isolated houses was it reasonable," it asked, "to drop 50 machine-guns on the off-chance that one would reach the insurrectionists? That is what, in the Russian view, the unfortunate British and Polish airmen, sent from England, did."

to widen the breach between the nationalistic aristocracy and the Polish peasantry or villagers.

The best indicator of the Polish agrarian structure at the present time is the general census of 1921 which, however, does not cover some districts in Upper Silesia and the Vilna voivodship. According to this census,—

		Percent of Total Area
Holdings of		
2 hectares,[8] and less, and 2-5 hectares } comprised		15.3
5-20 " "		31.8
20-100 " "		9.9
Over 100 " "		43.0

There is an interesting discussion of these figures in the *Journal of Central European Affairs*,[9] which states that

The statistics of 1921 indicate that the landholdings of 2 hectares and less constituted 34 per cent of the total amount of landholdings, with a population of five millions. These are the so-called dwarf holdings that cannot provide sufficient support for their owner and his family. 30.7 per cent of the landholdings are from 2 to 5 hectares, and a total population of almost 5 millions. Under Polish conditions, the majority of the farmers of this category cannot live from work on the land. The dominant figure of the Polish village was the poor peasant, with little property, not sufficient to provide himself and his family with sufficient support. *These two groups together constituted two-thirds of the agricultural population and owned only 15.3 per cent of the land.*[10] On the other hand, we have property holders of over 100 hectares, which property holders constitute a negligible percentage of all landholders—.6 per cent. But this handful of individuals owned almost half—43 per cent—of the total area.[11] In other words, in Poland there were a hundred times more poor peasants than rich landowners, the former possessing, together, only one-third of the land. . . . In this figure is expressed all the tragedy of the Polish

8. A *Hectare* is equal to 2.471 acres.

9. George Kagan, "Agrarian Regime of Pre-war Poland," in *Journal of Central European Affairs, Vol. 3*, October, 1943, pp. 247-248.

10. Italics ours.

11. Wladislaw R. Malinowski in his "Note on the Agrarian Regime of Post-War Poland," in *Journal of Central European Affairs*, Vol. 4, April, 1944, tries to bring in some corrections of Kagan's figures. Subtracting land not used for agricultural purposes, he comes to the conclusion that in 1921, not 43 but only 26.7 per cent consisted of large landholdings.

agrarian question: peasants without land on one side; land without laborers on the other.

Medium sized farms—20 to 100 hectares—played a very limited rôle in Poland. Leaving aside the Eastern voivodships, these farms had the characteristics of a capitalist economy, for they could not do without hired workers. The owners constituted 2.7 per cent of the total land-holders and they owned 9.3 per cent of the land.

After the restoration of Poland in 1919, some minor agrarian reforms were carried out, but they did not basically improve the condition of the peasant. The land reform laws of 1921 and 1925 benefited only a small number of well-to-do peasants, and the land owners were paid a high compensation for their estates. Nevertheless some progress was made. In its official bulletin, *Polish Facts and Figures*,[12] the Polish Government-in-exile stated that "during the twenty years of Poland's independence [from 1919 to 1939] more than six and one half million acres were parcelled among small farmers." This figure, however, gives no clear idea of the efficacy of the Polish land reform, since one learns that the amount was only about one-fourth of the area which poor peasants in Poland would receive under the projects outlined by the Polish Committee of National Liberation.

The claim of the Government-in-exile that "the present war prevented . . . Poland from completing her plan of agrarian reform" is therefore open to question. Actually all attempts at agrarian reform in Poland came to a stop in 1926 when Pilsudski came to power. He concluded the well-known *Nieswiezh* agreement with the landed aristocracy "with the result that in the years of his dictatorship the pace of land reform became even slower than before."[13] From an analysis of the history of restored Poland, it is therefore obvious that the outbreak of war in 1939 did not have any bearing upon the completion of a program of Polish agrarian reform. The interests of the Polish Government-in-exile were predominantly political, territorial and military, and in order to avoid dissension in its own ranks,— due to the presence of some landed aristocrats in the Government and in the National Council in London—it was averse to taking practical steps toward a solution of the agrarian issue. It is true, as has been mentioned above, that some attempts were made and some projects drafted in this direction; but no decisive action was taken by London Poles. In its last manifesto, toward the end of August, 1944, concerning "the democratic foundations of post-war Poland," the Government-in-exile issued the following narrow formula for agrarian legislation: *Land reform, by parceliza-*

---

12. *Polish Facts and Figures*, No. 9, September 25, 1944; published in New York by the Polish Government Information Center.

13. See *The Economist*, London, August 5, 1944.

tion of German-held property as well as of landed estates of more than 500 hectares (1236 acres).[14] Thus the long-overdue agrarian reform was transformed primarily into an anti-German issue. On the other hand, there can be little doubt that the moves by the Lublin Committee of Liberation towards the solution of the agrarian question would be enthusiastically acclaimed by the Polish peasantry. Especially noteworthy are the proposals of this Committee that no system of Soviet collective farming, of which the individualistic Polish peasant is so fearful, would be instituted or practiced. This stipulation cleverly takes into account the strength of the opposition, in Polish village life, to the practices of Bolshevization.[15] The effect of this pronouncement of the Lublin Committee upon the Polish masses exercised strong political and social influence, to the detriment of the prestige of the London Government.

EXCHANGE OF MINORITY POPULATIONS

Another no less important measure proposed by the Committee of Liberation is the exchange or transfer of minority populations. This means that the Ukrainians and the White Russians living west of the Russo-Polish border, conceived of as following the Curzon Line, would be transferred to their respective co-national Soviet Union Republics of the Ukraine and White Russia; and conversely, the Poles living to the east of the new border, in the Soviet Ukraine and in Soviet White Russia, would have the right to return or be transferred to new Poland.

Dispatches from Moscow stated that agreements providing for "voluntary transmigration" had been concluded between the Polish Committee of National Liberation and the governments of the Ukrainian and White Russian Soviet Socialist Republics. A question of grave consequence arose: whether any treaty-making power could be ascribed to the Committee. According to international law the only legally recognized body with authority to conclude treaties for Poland as a State was, at that time, the London Government-in-exile. Without doubt, the conclusion of these agreements by the Lublin Committee still further complicated the vexatious issues between it and the Government-in-exile.

14. Italics ours.
15. Notable in this connection, is the statement to the press made by Professor Lange on June 7, 1944, upon his return to the United States from the Soviet Union. He summed up the opinion of the soldiers of the Polish Army in Russia regarding the future needs of Poland as follows: "The soldiers are unanimous in demanding agrarian reform. They want the large estates divided among the peasants, but completely reject collectivization. Most soldiers want big industry and banking nationalized, and all soldiers demand private enterprise in small industry and trade. The officers and men of the Polish army in the U.S.S.R. want the solution of Poland's problems to grow out of the needs of Polish life and not to be based on an imitation of Soviet or any other foreign pattern." *Soviet Russia Today,* July, 1944.

Whatever the purely legalistic position of the agreements may be, fundamentally they follow precedents established by several internationally regulated transfers of populations. It will suffice to mention only two: the mutual exchange of Turkish and Greek minorities under the Treaty of Lausanne, of 1923, between Greece and Turkey; and the transfer of German minorities of Estonia and Latvia to Germany, under the Reich's treaty with Estonia of October 13, 1939, and with Latvia on October 30, 1939. It would be impossible, without studying the agreements themselves, to state to what degree the transmigration is "voluntary," that is, whether the option has been granted to every "transmigrant" to remain where he is or to remove to the territory of his "co-nationals."

This mutual exchange would tend to remove some old tensions between the Ukrainian minority and the Polish majority some distance west of the Curzon Line, tensions which had been used by the Czarist Government to weaken the position of the Poles in the Russian part of Poland, and, as a result of which a special non-Polish enclave district or "gubernia," Chelm, was created in the summer of 1912. Similar disruptive tendencies were manifested in Moscow just at the time when the London Polish Government was expected to make its decision concerning the acceptance or rejection of the Curzon Line. It was probably not a mere coincidence that a Ukrainian deputy made a speech in the Supreme Soviet reiterating the pre-war claim for the Ukrainization of four districts: Chelm, Hrubieszow, Zamosc and Jaroslav, all of them being ethnically Polish territory to the west of the Curzon Line.

Fundamentally, however, the agreements are much more humanitarian and show much greater consideration for the welfare of the people exchanged than was the case in the Balkan and Baltic transfers cited above, and especially for those who will, of their own choice, be assigned to lands for individual farming. It remains to be seen what if any rights will be granted by the Soviet Union to Ukrainian and White Russian immigrants from provinces inside Poland, such as Chelm and Western Galicia, to the Soviet Ukraine and to Soviet White Russia. Under the agreements, property, both movable and immovable, left behind by the immigrants will be paid for in accordance with the laws of Poland and of the two Soviet Republics.

In fact, the first trainload of Poles transferred from White Russia to Poland left Grodno, Baranowicze, and other important White Russian towns, in December, 1944. Representatives of the Polish Committee of National Liberation were rounding up Poles in White Russia and arranging for their return to Poland. A similar voluntary evacuation of Poles, from Lwow and its surrounding districts, began even earlier.

As to the general attitude to the problem of the transfer of populations in order to create ethnically unified territories on both sides of the Curzon Line, in the east, and between Poles and Germans on the west, Mr. Churchill for the first time gave full approbation in an unequivocal statement before the House of Commons, on December 15, 1944:

> There will be no mixture of population to cause endless struggle, as in Alsace-Lorraine. A clear sweep will be made. I am not alarmed at the prospect of the disentanglement of population, nor even am I alarmed by those large transferences which are more possible than they ever were before, through modern conditions. . . . I cannot see any doubt whatever that the Great Powers, if they agree, can effect this transference of population.

The transfer of minority populations in both western and eastern Poland is but one instance of a series of such transfers brought about by the second World War. At the Potsdam Conference the heads of the three governments decided that the "transfer to Germany of German populations, or elements thereof, remaining in Poland, Czechoslovakia and Hungary, will have to be undertaken . . . in an orderly and humane manner."[16]

DISPARITIES IN THE POLISH POLITICAL SITUATION

Recent Russo-Polish relations have suffered from clashes resulting from growing mistrust and misunderstanding between the Polish Government-in-exile and the Polish Committee of National Liberation. As the controversy developed, the sponsors for either side—Great Britain and the United States for the Government-in-exile, and the Soviet Union for the Lublin Committee—became increasingly enmeshed in the political tangle. The great disparities in Polish political thought and institutions appeared more sharply with the advance of Red Army occupation of Poland. Duality was manifested in the existence side by side of:

1. The two Polish Undergrounds: one connected with the London Government and subject to its orders; the other subject to the Committee of Liberation.

2. The two armies: one connected with the Soviet supreme command; the other collaborating with the western Allies in and beyond Poland.

3. The two Governments, each with a President, and their respective advisory councils or parliaments, representing basically one and the same subject of international law, the Polish State.

4. The two Constitutions: that of 1921 and the other of 1935, from

16. See Section XIII on the Report of the Tripartite Conference of Berlin. *New York Times*, August 3, 1945.

which the two regimes derive their rights and their connection with and succession to pre-war Poland.

5. And, as a consequence of the above, the dualism and rivalry in the field of international law and foreign relations of two treaty-making powers: the London Government which negotiated the first treaties with the Soviet Union, and the Lublin Committee with which the Soviet Union made its last agreements on the exchange of minority populations.

To all the tragedies of war and occupation, of which Poland has probably been the greatest European victim, there is now added the most tragic circumstance, that of Polish internal dissension. While most other European nations are returning to their pre-war existence united (in some cases uneasily so) in allegiance to their Governments, there is division in Poland in the matter of her very acceptance of the idea of national liberation. This is the greatest tragedy of all. It is a partition of Poland by the Poles, and comes from within Poland itself, in contrast with the external partition, towards the close of the eighteenth century, by Russia, Prussia, and Austria.

Developments Preceding the Moscow Conference

On September 28, 1944, in his speech before the House of Commons, Prime Minister Churchill, while placing reliance upon Premier Mikolajczyk's willingness to reach a friendly understanding and settlement with Soviet Russia, gave British support to the Soviet Union's territorial claims on the ground that Russia was "entitled to safe frontiers and to have friendly neighbors on her western flank." He added, however, a note of somber realism in a warning not to minimize the extent of Soviet-Polish tension as a serious international issue and made clear the independent stand of the British Government and also, as he ventured to indicate, of the United States Government. All the elements of this complicated problem were brought to mind in the terms in which he referred to the dispute at that time.

It would [he said], be an affectation to pretend that the attitude of the British Government, and I believe of the United States Government, toward Poland is identical with that of the Soviet Union. Every allowance must be made for different conditions of history and of geography which govern the relationship of the Western Democracies on the one hand and of the Soviet Government on the other, with the Polish nation.

On the same day the Polish Government-in-exile took a step which was interpreted at the time as designed to conciliate Moscow. By a unanimous decision of the Polish Government-in-exile General Sosnkowski was relieved of the post of Commander-in-Chief of the Polish Army despite the reluctance of President Wladyslaw Rackiewicz. General Tadeusz Komorowski, commander of the Polish Underground "Home Army" and leader of the Warsaw uprising, was appointed as his successor. For some days after this action by the Polish Government-in-exile it was hoped that this gesture would facilitate the long-delayed settlement of the Soviet-Polish dispute, but this possibility was at once destroyed by the statement of Edward Osubka-Morawski, chairman of the Polish Committee of Liberation, who attacked General Komorowski as "having committed a crime against the Polish People," when he ordered the uprising prematurely. There was also a demand in Moscow government circles for the removal of President Rackiewicz. The breach widened still further when, on October 3, 1944, Komorowski and his insurgent army in Warsaw surrendered to the Nazis after sixty-three days of bitter resistance. When the first news of this surrender was given out by the Germans the Lublin Poles spread the charge that Komorowski himself had escaped, leaving his men to their fate. Adding insult to injury, they declared as well that the surrender was intentional and a friendly, pro-German act. The London Poles were soon able to publish a denial of this charge when Komorowski's capture was formally announced. Nevertheless, the Germans took advantage of the situation to display for the time being a pro-Polish attitude. The insurgents were declared regular prisoners of war and at the time were treated accordingly. In other words, they were not shot when they surrendered, which was the common fate of the prisoners from the Underground forces when captured by the Germans during their five years of occupation. This pro-Polish policy, however, did not last for long.

This otherwise incredible situation is only explicable as having grown out of an earlier charge by the pro-Soviet Poles against the so-called "Home Army" uprising. In an article in *The War and the Working Class* for June 15, 1944, we find the following charges made against the London Poles and General Bor, or Komorowski:

> After the provocation of Katyn [the alleged murder of the Polish officers by Russians] the Germans informed the Home Army of the London Poles that they, the Germans, would not oppose the organization of military units to fight with them against the invading Red Army. General Grot, the head of the Home Army at that time, declined these proposals and was immediately imprisoned by the Germans. General Bor, who replaced Grot, co-operated with the Germans and formed special units to fight against Soviet and Polish partisans. This took place eighteen months ago [at the beginning of 1943]. Thus the Government-in-exile used its armed forces in Poland to fight along with the Germans against

Polish partisans whom they called "bandits," instead of leading the Poles to fight the Germans.

In contrast with this regrettable record of strife between the anti-Soviet and pro-Soviet Polish leaders it should be said that the population as a whole has maintained a commendable spirit of national self-consciousness. There are no indications of there having been any real sympathy with the Nazi authorities, and almost no evidence of any willingness to co-operate with them during the entire period of the occupation. It should be a matter of real pride to the Poles that no Quisling was ever found among them. Compared with some of the other occupied States where there were considerable local Nazi movements, Poland remained adamant against any mass penetration by Nazism in spite of the fact that in the five years prior to the invasion, or from 1934 to 1939, under Pilsudski and his successors, there had been a pro-German orientation of Polish policy. It is true that there were some pro-Nazi, anti-semitic elements among the people such as the collaborationists Kozlowski, a former Prime Minister, Trzeciak, a priest, Alfred Wysocki, and a few others; but these constituted a negligible fraction of the Polish population.

There was further evidence of this stability of Polish conduct and the innate integrity of the Polish people in their refusal to be deceived by an eleventh hour change of heart upon the part of the Nazis who, as was usual with them, crudely overdid their appeal to the Poles, going so far as to stage memorial services for the Warsaw dead. A fair sample of Nazi "repentance" is to be found in a statement of the Posen *Ost-deutscher Beobachter*, designed to win over the Poles at the darkest moment of the long, tragic struggle. The statement said in part:

> Abandoned by England and threatened by Moscow which does not even deign to answer the notes of Poland's Government-in-exile, the people of the Polish nation now turn in desperation to their ostensible "enemy" to appeal for understanding. If their appeal proves to have been made in full loyalty there is no reason whatsoever why Berlin should turn a deaf ear.[17]

This appeal, however, was not accompanied by even the slightest concession to Polish political integrity in any proffer from the German Government, and the "humanitarian" episode proved short-lived. On October 19, 1944, the Polish Government-in-exile informed the world that the Germans had not kept their promise to treat captured members of the Polish Home Army as prisoners of war, but had begun mass executions of them in gas chambers at the *Oswiecim* and *Brzesinka* concentration camps.

17. This statement is quoted in the *New York Times*, October 7, 1944.

A final comment should be added. This study deals with the problems of the relations of Poland with Soviet Russia, not with its relations with Germany. However, it may be well to recall that the Nazis made no such efforts as were made by Germany from time to time to win over the Poles, much less extend such political favors as were given the Poles by the Kaiser's Germany and Hapsburg Austria. Such policies, to say nothing of promises to restore Poland politically, would have been in open contradiction to the doctrine of *Mein Kampf*. Nazi Germany's attitude towards the Slavs, and in particular toward the Poles, was clearly stated by Greiser, the Gauleiter of the occupied Polish district of Warthegau, at Inowraclaw, early in June, 1944, when he said that if the Poles behaved themselves they would be guaranteed "work, bread, and a roof over their heads," a promise tempting only to slaves, but utterly without appeal to a heroic nation.

MR. CHURCHILL GOES TO MOSCOW

By October, 1944, it became evident that the rift between Moscow and the Polish Government-in-exile was developing dangerously. The situation was rendered still more difficult by the fact that in the United States the controversy was carried into American domestic politics in a presidential election. The leaders in this movement were chiefly Americans of Polish ancestry of whom there are very many, especially in the industrial centers of New York, Boston, Detroit, Chicago and Pittsburgh. American sympathy for Poles is, however, not limited by any means to Americans of Polish descent. From the days of Pulaski and Kosciuszko, in the Revolutionary War, all through American history, there has been a strong and romantic sentiment toward Poland. This sentiment is bound to affect American policy to some extent, as is evident in the interest of both presidential candidates in Poland's case.

Governor Dewey addressed a great gathering of Poles in New York on Pulaski Day, October 8, 1944. His remarks were not confined to the general support of Poles fighting for political restoration but touched specifically upon matters of territorial settlement, going so far as to state that the American people recognize the justice of the claims urged by the great Polish pianist and patriot, Jan I. Paderewski. Literally interpreted, this would mean that Poland's territory must be restored to the old borders, far to the east of the Curzon Line.

President Roosevelt received a delegation of members of the Polish American Congress headed by Charles Rozmarek, on October 11, 1944. This delegation, purporting to represent six millions of Americans of Polish descent, definitely asked for the President's support for Poland's demand for the borders of 1921 to 1939. In this it showed itself even more radically nationalist than the Government-in-exile which had conceded to the U.S.S.R. some provisional adjustments of the frontier during the war and a possible arrangement based on plebiscites in Eastern Poland after the war. The delegates at Washington categorically rejected both frontier revisions and plebiscites, and also, contrary to the London Poles, showed no hesitancy in demanding for Poland East Prussia and Upper Silesia from Germany, Vilna from Lithuania, and Teschen from Czechoslovakia.

President Roosevelt assured the delegation that Poland must be reconstituted as a strong and independent nation, but was careful to avoid the territorial question. It should be recalled that the phrase "a strong and independent nation" had been Stalin's phrase as well. The delegation requested the President to make a public statement on the matter, but no such statement was forthcoming.

In this connection it should be understood that there is no record of similar delegations to President Roosevelt by Americans of Ukrainian or White Russian extraction for the purpose of presenting their views or making demands upon the American Government to take sides in this question, although a great majority of the population in the territory in dispute are their kinsmen.

In the midst of this confusion and attempted intervention which threatened to create a serious situation in the relations of the "Big Three" came the announcement of Prime Minister Churchill's visit to Moscow to consult with Marshal Stalin. The conference was ostensibly called to deal with the co-ordination of policies between Soviet Russia and its Allies in southeastern Europe and elsewhere, as well as those affecting Poland. This made it possible for Mr. Churchill to intervene in the Polish dispute without seeming to have had any definite plan to do so, which is a well-recognized technique in diplomacy. The conference began with only British and Russian members conferring, and the American Ambassador present as observer. After the initial stages of negotiation the Prime Minister of Poland was invited to come from London and join in the discussion. Undoubtedly the Polish problem had been previously explored by both Governments, for otherwise there would not have been any special reason for extending the invitation to Premier Mikolajczyk.

The dispatches stated that the basis of the conference of the three statesmen would be the memorandum which had been sent by Premier Mikolajczyk to Marshal Stalin some six weeks earlier, on his return to London after his previous visit to Moscow. In this memorandum Mikolajczyk proposed that there should be a new Polish government, which should include the Communists as well as the four major parties, but exclude the factions associated with the pre-1939 Warsaw regime;[18] that there should be a new democratic constitution and social and agrarian reforms; that the new Poland should co-operate with Soviet Russia in the war against Germany and in postwar economic planning, and, finally, that there should be an amicable settlement of the frontier controversy.[19]

Moscow Negotiations

The negotiations got off to a promising start on October 13th and, according to the communiqué, Stalin and Churchill made a determined bid for unity between the Polish groups of London and Lublin, both represented at the meeting. This effort failed, however. The Moscow-supported Lublin group demanded recognition of equality with the Government-in-exile which at least technically could not be granted. Then the agrarian problem came to the fore. The Lublin group asserted that their effort at agrarian reform in liberated Poland had been sabotaged by pro-Pilsudski and other conservative elements which had filtered into the land councils and which were loyal to the London Government-in-exile. Following that, the Lublin Minister of Agriculture, Andrej Witos, was relieved of his post. It should be recalled, however, in this connection that the territory in question had only been recovered from German occupation a few short weeks before and that therefore any considerable agrarian project could not possibly have been carried out at that time.

On the question of Communism, if the dispatches are correct, Mr. Churchill agreed with the proposal of Mikolajczyk that the Communist Party of Poland be accepted in the Government on an equal footing with the other four parties. But Stalin could not consent to this without disavowing the Lublin Liberation Committee created by Moscow; and this again brought to the fore the organizational differences between the two Polish groups and pushed aside the really fundamental political issues in the dispute.

Among these organizational problems was the question of whether the Lublin group should have diplomatic representation. It proposed as its representative in London one Stefan Wilanowski, but as Great Britain had

18. On the Polish political parties see pages 25-31, above.
19. At the conferences the London Polish Government-in-exile was represented by Premier Mikolajczyk, Foreign Minister Tadeusz Romer, and Dr. Stanislaw Grabski, speaker of the Polish Council; the Lublin Poles were represented by their chairman, Edward Osubka-Morawski, President Boleslaw Bierut, and General Michal Rola-Zymierski of the Polish Committee of National Liberation.

At a meeting with Premier Stalin, Mr. Grabski sat down next to the Premier and began shouting out Poland's claims to Lwow and Vilna. Other members of the Polish delegation were afraid that Stalin would be displeased, but instead he said, "You are a very good propagandist. I enjoyed it." See R. E. Lauterbach, *These Are the Russians*, Harper's, 1945, pp. 117-118.

already recognized the cabinets of the Polish Government-in-exile it was apparent even during the conversations at Moscow that it would have no official dealings with Wilanowski. The Moscow-sponsored group thus found itself in a less advantageous position and was compelled to compromise, so that by the close of the negotiations the Polish groups came closer together. A tentative understanding was finally reached. This was stated by a spokesman for the Mikolajczyk delegation as follows: "We expect it will be only a matter of weeks before both Polish camps start working together in Poland."

As the negotiations drew to a close it became clear that the Polish question had not been settled in any of its major aspects. Moreover, according to Polish constitutional precepts, the Polish delegation in Moscow could not reach a final agreement without a mandate from the Polish Government in London. On the other hand the Soviets made it plain that they had reached a final decision and would not yield on the frontier of the Curzon Line, proposing that German territory to the west and north of Poland be given in exchange. In an official communiqué[20] a brief resumé of the Soviet-Polish *pourparlers* was given in somewhat optimistic tone:

> Important progress was made toward solution of the Polish question, which was closely discussed between the Soviet and British Governments. These discussions have notably narrowed differences and dispelled misconceptions.[21]

From the published reports and from Mr. Churchill's statement in Parliament it is clear that Mr. Mikolajczyk did not take back to London any formula for settlement. Indeed, it would seem more likely that as the war drew to its end Soviet unwillingness to make any concession on the Curzon Line was strengthened rather than lessened. Under these circumstances the serious consequences of a refusal by the Poles to make concessions were commented upon in some sections of the American press. Yet the more conservative and nationalistic circles of the London Poles remained fully as stubborn and unyielding as the Soviet authorities. Fortunately this opinion was not shared by all the London Poles because, as Mr. Churchill stated in his speech before Parliament, he still entertained hopes that the Polish Government-in-exile would reach an agreement with Moscow.

The detailed record of the Moscow conference is, of course, not available,

20. *New York Times*, October 22, 1944.

21. It should not be forgotten that after the rupture of diplomatic relations between the Polish Government-in-exile and the Soviet Union, in April, 1943, there have been no direct official negotiations between them. This may explain why this optimistic summary does not mention directly the then apparent betterment of relations between Poland and the Soviet Union.

but fortunately in this instance, as in so many others, the British system of government calls for a statement to Parliament of any major commitments made or attempted by its Government. Therefore Prime Minister Churchill gave a frank and clear statement to Parliament on October 27 of what took place at Moscow. As this marks a definite milestone in the history of the dispute, Mr. Churchill's account of his effort at a settlement should be given in his own words:

The most urgent and burning question was, of course, that of Poland, and here again I speak words of hope reinforced by confidence. To abandon hope in this matter would indeed be to surrender to despair.

In this sphere there are two issues, two critical issues. The first is the question of the eastern frontier of Poland with Russia and the Curzon Line, as it is called, and new territories to be added to Poland in the north and west. This is the first issue, and the second is the relation of the Polish Government with the Lublin National Liberation Committee.

On these two points, apart from many necessary ancillary points—on these two main points we held a series of conferences with both parties. We held them together and saw them separately, and, of course, we were in constant discussion with the heads of the Soviet Government.

I had several very long talks with Marshal Stalin, and the Foreign Secretary was every day working on these and cognate matters with Mr. Molotoff. Two or three times we all four met together with no one but interpreters present.

I wish I could tell the House we had reached a solution of these problems. It certainly is not for the want of trying. I am quite sure, however, that we have got a great deal nearer to it. I hope Mr. Mikolajczyk will soon return to Moscow, and it will be a great disappointment to all sincere friends of Poland if a good arrangement cannot be made which will enable him to form a Polish Government on Polish soil, a Government recognized by all the great powers concerned and, indeed, by all those Governments of the United Nations which now recognize only the Polish Government in London.

Although I do not underrate the difficulties which remain, it is a comfort to feel that Britain and Soviet Russia and, I do not doubt, the United States, are all firmly agreed in the re-creation of a strong, free, independent sovereign Poland, loyal to the Allies, and friendly to her great neighbor and liberator Russia.

Speaking more particularly for His Majesty's Government, it is our persevering and constant aim that the Polish people after their suffering and vicissitudes shall find in Europe an abiding home and resting place, which, though it may not entirely coincide or correspond with the prewar frontier of Poland, will nevertheless be adequate for the needs of the Polish nation and not inferior in character or in quality, taking the picture as a whole, to what they had previously possessed.

These are critical days and it would be a great pity if time were wasted in indecisions or in protracted negotiations. If the Polish Government had taken the advice we tendered them at the beginning of this year, the additional complication produced by the formation of the Polish National Committee of Liberation at Lublin would never have arisen.

Anything like a prolonged delay in settlement can only have the effect of increasing the division between the Poles in London and the Poles in Warsaw and hampering a common action which the Poles and Russians and the rest of the Allies are taking against Germany. Therefore, I hope no time will be lost in continuing these discussions and pressing on to an effective conclusion.[22]

From this account it is evident that, as noted above, although Premier Mikolajczyk did not yield in Moscow, there were still hopes that the Polish Government-in-exile would accept the inevitable establishment of the Curzon Line—for the British Government continued to support the Soviet territorial claims—and would use the occasion to negotiate for compensation, both territorial and political, before it was too late. The *New York Times* correspondent, cabling from London on October 27, 1944, stated that:

A large and strong body of Poles would prefer not to give legal recognition to the loss of eastern Poland by the Government's formal signature, preferring to allow the Russians to take its possession without approval.

This view, however, is not likely to prevail, particularly since Britain is ready to guarantee the sovereignty of the new Poland. Polish authorities hope for assurance by the United States that the guarantee will mean no foreign interference.

The Poles also want a promise of United Nations aid in restoring her economy in the new Poland and in resettling as many of the 12,000,000 persons in eastern Poland who may wish to move to avoid Russian authority. The Poles estimate at least 6,000,000 will move.

This comment of the newspaper correspondent obviously reflects the then unpublished conclusions of the Polish Government-in-exile concerning the Moscow Conference. There is, of course, no way of judging how many of those living east of the Curzon Line will want to move into Poland, but from the analysis of the previous pages of this study it seems by no means

22. *New York Times*, Oct. 28, 1944.

likely that there will be a vast migration of the peasantry to escape incorporation in Soviet Russia. Certainly this will not be the case if Soviet Russia carries out agrarian reforms and the Polish Government continues to withhold them. It is almost inevitable that a Government-in-exile should concentrate its attention upon military and political matters, while those at home are more interested in securing a better way of living. This fact is growing apparent in the case of occupied territories other than Poland.

7. The Yalta Conference

MR. CHURCHILL'S visit to Moscow was viewed with disquiet in the circles supporting the Polish Government-in-exile, both in the United States and in England. The Polish Government refused to accept any settlement of the eastern boundary without a definite settlement at the same time of accessions of territory in East Prussia, Pomerania and Silesia, and a guarantee that Poland's independence would be respected within the new frontiers.

About this time there appeared dissension between the Peasant Party of Mikolajczyk and the other party groups supporting the London Government, which grew hourly. The Peasant Party remained more consistent in the attempt to reach a compromise with Moscow than the Socialist Party which, in general political questions, was more radical than the Peasant Party. Only Jan Stanczyk, a Socialist, and a representative of the labor unions, joined the Peasants in the opposition. The National Democrats and the non-Partisan members, with the partial support of the Socialists, were violently opposed to all attempts by their Premier to negotiate a compromise with Moscow after his return to London for further consultation with his Government. The result of this split was that on November 24, 1944, Mr. Mikolajczyk resigned as Premier of Poland. This step was fateful for the London Government. Despite the rupture of diplomatic relations with Moscow, the London Government was a going political concern so long as it was in practical negotiations with Moscow, Downing Street and Washington. Moreover, Mr. Mikolajczyk was the only man in the London Polish Government and its supporting groups acceptable to the Kremlin as the head of a government combining the Government-in-exile and the Lublin group which at that time was increasingly taking on the character of a Polish Government on the spot. His resignation foreshadowed the twilight of the Exile Government and its relegation to a token existence. True, Jan Kwapinski, a Socialist, was designated by President Rackiewicz to form another Cabinet, but Mikolajczyk's party refused to enter the new Government.

On November 30th, after the failure of Kwapinski, a new Polish Cabinet in exile took office under the premiership of the Socialist leader, Tomascz

Arciszewski. This Government was formed without any representatives of the Peasant Party, Poland's largest, and three positions were left open for the Peasants without being filled. The situation of the London Polish Government became steadily more isolated and powerless. Even with the formal recognition of the regime by Great Britain and the United States there was no real contact between the London Poles and the British Prime Minister or members of the British Government. This isolation was accentuated by the growing opposition of the Exile Government to the Lublin Poles, who finally decided, about the middle of December, 1944, to reorganize their Committee into a full-fledged Provisional Government and to take all necessary steps for carrying out social reforms, and particularly the agrarian reform.

Churchill's speech, delivered on December 15, 1944, can now in historic perspective be considered the last warning directed to the Exile Government to waste no more time and to find a compromise with Moscow on the basis of the Curzon Line before further and final decisions were made. The Prime Minister quite frankly expressed his displeasure over the stand taken by the London Poles after Mikolajczyk's return from Moscow. He said, we repeat,

> If the Polish Government had taken the advice we tendered at the beginning of this year, the additional complications produced by the formation of the Polish National Committee of Liberation at Lublin would not have arisen.

This was, in reality, a thought he had often expressed, and it was directed primarily at the Government-in-exile. The Prime Minister also said, in the same speech, that Mr. Mikolajczyk's efforts and his good will made him "more qualified to fill the place of the late General Sikorski than any other of the Polish leaders." And, finally, there was a direct challenge to the London Poles in the Prime Minister's remarks (again we repeat):

> I hope Mr. Mikolajczyk will soon return to Moscow and it will be a great disappointment to the sincere friends of Poland if an agreed arrangement cannot be made which will enable him to form a Polish Government on Polish soil, a Government recognized by the Great Powers and indeed by all the Governments of the United Nations which now recognize the Polish Government in London.

He emphasized the fact that Poland would get in exchange for land east of the Curzon Line all of East Prussia south and west of Koenigsberg, the important port of Danzig, and a Baltic Sea front of 200 miles. He also gave his full approval to the compulsory transfer of populations to avoid a mixture of Germans and Poles.[1]

In order to bring about a positive attitude of the London Poles before the next conference of the Big Three, Prime Minister Churchill frankly invited the United States to clarify its position. He did not say that the hopes of the London Poles and their Government were based mainly on the assurance of American support in their frontier dispute with Russia, but circumvented the point by stating that

> The friendship of the United States Government for Poland, no less than our own, the large mass of Poles who have made their homes in the United States . . . all these have not enabled the Government of that great nation to speak in terms which I have thought it my duty to use in this House.

This challenge of Mr. Churchill had some repercussions in the United States, and led to the statement by Secretary of State Stettinius concerning Poland, issued on December 18, 1944, in which reference was made to the traditional policy of the United States of declining to give guarantees for specific frontiers. At the same time, however, the Secretary declared, the Government "stands unequivocally for a strong, free and independent Polish state." As for the boundaries, Paragraph II of the Secretary's statement provides that "questions relating to boundaries should be left in abeyance until the termination of hostilities." Nevertheless, the assertion in this statement that the Government is ready to assist Poland in the transfer of certain national groups if the people of Poland "decide that it would be in the interests of the Polish state," leaves no doubt about the positive attitude of the United States toward the territorial enlargement of Poland in the west and toward changes along the Curzon Line.

In the last weeks of 1944, the Lublin Committee sought recognition as the provisional government of Poland, in open repudiation of the Government-in-exile. Thereupon the Polish Provisional Government was formed, and Boleslaw Bierut was named the President. Edward Osubka-Morawski was nominated Prime Minister and Minister of Foreign Affairs, and General Michal Rola-Zymierski, Minister of Defense and Commander-in-chief.

Without question this action had the approval of the U.S.S.R., and would not have been taken without it. It provoked the most vehement protests on the part of the Government-in-exile which branded the Lublin regime as having been introduced by the coercive action of a foreign-sponsor. The United States and Great Britain then announced that they would continue to give diplomatic recognition to the Polish Government-

1. See Chapter VI, "The Exchange of Minority Populations."

in-exile. Both Governments tried to defer the whole question of recognition until it could be considered at a joint meeting of Great Britain, the United States, and the Soviet Union. The Soviet Government, however, gave official recognition to the Lublin Provisional Government on January 5, 1945. In this it was followed by Czechoslovakia which did not, however, break off diplomatic relations with the Polish Government. President Benes properly enough thus kept the field open for future usefulness in diplomatic negotiations. France sent a special diplomatic agent to the Lublin Government.

It became apparent in early February, 1945, that President Roosevelt would submit a plan at the forthcoming conference of the Big Three of a compromise settlement, involving the removal of both the extremists in London and in the Lublin Polish Government, and the formation of a new coalition government on broader democratic lines.

The Lublin Government had the advantage of being on the spot and close to the needs and the plight of the country, a situation of which the London Poles themselves were compelled to take cognizance. This factual situation was particularly aggravated by the further liberation by the U.S.S.R. of large regions of Poland. Although the London Government, following the resignation of Mikolajczyk and the installation of the Arciszewski Cabinet, put great stress upon the importance of the Home Army, it was forced by the development of events to dissolve that Army some weeks later, on February 7. On the other hand, to the new local Government of Lublin accrued all the advantages of starting reforms and establishing a new administration.

From the standpoint of international relations the situation was at an impasse. A deadlock had been reached by the two bodies, one of which from the beginning of the war had been recognized as the legal government of Poland, and the other of which had been gradually established in the later stages of the war, with the sponsorship of the Soviet Union and some Polish social groups behind it.

Out of this difficulty the Yalta Conference found a way based upon the American proposal that both regimes be dropped and a new provisional government of Poland be established.

The text of the decision reached by the three Great Powers at the Yalta (Crimean) Conference regarding Poland is set out in full in Annex VI. The most important points of the decision are as follows:

1. The establishment of a Polish Provisional Government which can be more broadly based than was possible before the recent liberation of western Poland . . . with the inclusion of democratic leaders from Poland itself and from Poles abroad.

2. This Polish Provisional Government of National Unity shall be pledged to the holding of free and unfettered elections as soon as possible on the basis of universal suffrage and secret ballot.

3. [The appointment of an international Commission] to consult . . . with members of the present Provisional Government and other Polish democratic leaders from within Poland and from abroad with a view to the reorganization of the present Government along the above lines. [On this Commission the U.S.S.R. was to have one representative, M. Molotoff, while the United States was to be represented by Mr. Harriman and Great Britain by Sir A. Clark Kerr.]

4. When a Polish Provisional Government of National Unity has been properly formed in conformity with the above, [the three Great Powers represented at the Conference] will establish diplomatic relations with the new Polish Provisional Government of National Unity and will exchange Ambassadors. . . .

5. The three heads of Government consider that the eastern frontier of Poland should follow the Curzon Line, with digressions from it in some regions of five to eight kilometers in favor of Poland.

6. Poland must receive substantial accessions of territory in the north and west.

7. The opinion of the new Polish Provisional Government of National Unity should be sought in due course on the extent of these accessions.

8. The final delimitation of the western frontier of Poland should thereafter await the peace conference.

It will at once be seen that the Yalta agreement subordinated the territorial problem to the central one of the nature and composition of the future Polish Government itself. American public opinion not only applauded this method of dealing with the two problems together but was especially happy to note that there were to be American and British members on the Commission appointed to supervise the establishment of a "new Provisional Government of National Unity." This concession on the part of Moscow was regarded as generous and far sighted, and a guarantee that the frequent references to the "independence" of Poland were not merely a form of words. But this initial reaction in the United States to the Yalta agreement was tempered by a continuing doubt as to whether the promises would be lived up to, a doubt which grew as time went on.

Unfortunately, the parts to be played by the rival regimes—the Government-in-exile and the Lublin Provisional Government—in the formation of a "Polish Provisional Government of National Unity" were not made sufficiently clear in the document, which simply states that "the Provisional Government which is now functioning in Poland should . . . be reorganized on a broader democratic basis with the inclusion of democratic leaders from Poland itself and from Poles abroad." It does not specifically mention the Government-in-exile. From the context, the new Government of National Unity would appear to be only a reorganization of the Lublin Provisional Government and not a political welding of the two Polish Governments. It must be recalled that as yet the British and American Governments continued to recognize the Polish London Government as the only legal government of Poland.[2] On the other hand, as the record shows, Moscow, having broken off relations with the London Government, turned to the Lublin body, which had promptly moved to Warsaw.

It may have been politically impossible at the time to have a more precise text with reference to the new Government of Poland. The nature and composition of that body was not specified because an international Commission was appointed to deal with it. The postponement, however, was a mistake. The lack of clarity with reference to the nature of the new Polish Government became in turn a lack of clarity as to the function of the international Commission itself.

With reference to the settlement of the frontiers of Poland, the Big Three took note in their deliberations of the difference in character between the frontiers on the east from those on the west. It was considered by them "that the eastern frontier of Poland should follow the Curzon Line, with digressions from it in some regions of five to eight kilometers in favor of Poland."[3] This decision was based on the ethnographical situation in respect to which the attitude of the United States remained substantially the same from the time of President Wilson's Fourteen Points to President Roosevelt's report to Congress on the Yalta Conference, on March 1, 1945, in which he said,

> It is well known that the people east of the Curzon Line are predominantly White Russian and Ukrainian. They are not Polish, to a very great majority. And the people west of the Line are predominantly Polish.

The "substantial accessions of territory in the north and west," which are

2. In a speech delivered February 28, 1945, in the House of Commons, Mr. Eden explained why it was impossible to "derecognize" both the London and the Lublin governments for the sake of equality. The Soviet Union's objection to it was that "they must have some authority on their lines of communication through Poland, whether we like or dislike the Lublin Committee." It was agreed that both the governments would continue to be recognized—London by the Anglo-Americans and Lublin by Russia—"pending the creation of the new [provisional] Government." (Cables to the British Information Services, New York.)

3. On August 16, 1945, Russia and Poland signed a treaty which fixed their common boundary along the Curzon Line, except for deviations from three to almost nineteen miles in favor of the Poles. The delimitation of the border by a mixed commission will start within fifteen days of ratification. *New York Times*, August 18, 1945. See map, page xxxx.

conceded to Poland in the decision, include East Prussia, a stretch of the
Baltic Sea front, and Silesia. Here the ethnographical predominance of
Polish majority is to be found only in some areas. These regions once belonged to Poland before it was partitioned by Prussia, Russia and Austria
in the eighteenth century.[4] With the development of nationalism in the
nineteenth century, accompanied by imperialism on the part of both Russia and Germany, the Polish people in their territories were obliged to submit to policies of denationalization, their children were denied education
in the Polish language, and the effort was made, though with but varying
success, to deprive them of their lands. Austria did not join in this policy,
partly because of the decentralization of the Austrian Empire and partly
because of the lack of aggressive, anti-nationalist, imperialist policies at that
time.

Viewed in the light of history, in which light the Polish nationalists view
it, the extension of Polish territory on the west would be the undoing of
an ancient wrong, taking back into Poland land which had been seized by
Prussia in the partitions. But all history shows that ancient wrongs cannot
be easily redressed if in the course of generations new societies are born
with new roots in the soil. Only the soil remains unchanged and even it may
wholly change its uses as in the case of industrial Silesia, a land of peasant
farmers up to the days of Frederick the Great, now a busy hive of industry
as well.

The proposal to extend Polish territories to the west and north in compensation for the loss on the east also brings up in a major form the extremely difficult problem of the transfer of populations. We have dealt with
this problem in general terms earlier in this study, but much more remains
to be said about it than is possible here. Compulsory migration is not a
mere formula to enable diplomats or governments to escape from difficult
situations. It raises problems which cannot be solved by merely looking at
the map. We have seen during the war the sufferings involved in migrations
forced by military necessity or by conquest. The migrations in the postwar
settlement would lack the ruthless quality of these acts of war, but they
would still cause much suffering on the part of the dispossessed. We are
speaking here only of forced migration, and the comment would not apply
to the movement of peoples under plebiscite or by agreement.

We are, however, anticipating at this stage of our study, because as President Roosevelt pointed out, the final delimitations of Poland's western
border were not fixed at Yalta but were left "to await the peace conference."

4. *The Economist* (London), February 10, 1945, mentions plans to extend Poland to
the old Polish provinces of Pomerania and Brandenburg in the following words: "The
'Study Section' of the Lublin department for the Western Areas has now put out a plan
claiming a frontier 30 miles to the west of the Oder, so that the river may be a waterway
for Silesia."

Nowhere else in the official literature of postwar conferences is there a reference to "the peace conference." This may have been a careless method of reference; or it may have been a slip, revealing further major plans of which we as yet know nothing.

While public opinion in the United States and in the United Kingdom gave full endorsement to most of the conclusions of the Yalta Conference, it was strongly divided on the issue of Poland. The British Prime Minister and the Foreign Secretary both reacted strongly in their speeches to Parliament against the criticisms of "an eloquent minority" of Conservatives, Liberals and Laborites in the House of Commons[5] who attacked the agreement as a surrender to Moscow. These critics were concerned for the security and independence of Poland and the inviolability of her previous frontiers, and protested against the ill-treatment of the London Government-in-exile in these matters. Sir William Beveridge also raised the question of the "unrealistic policy of dismembering and impoverishing Germany."

In his report to the House of Commons on the Yalta Conference decisions, February 27, 1945, Mr. Churchill took basically the same position which he had defended in Parliament, on December 15, 1944, prior to Yalta. In regard to the territorial issue he pointed out that

> The three Powers are agreed that the acceptance by the Poles of the provisions of the eastern frontiers, and so far as now can be ascertained on the western frontiers, is an essential condition of the establishment and future welfare of a strong, independent, homogeneous Polish State.

In most interesting, frank and detailed parliamentary declarations in the House of Commons (February 28, 1945) Foreign Secretary Eden denied vigorously that Britain ever had guaranteed Poland's eastern, pre-war frontiers. He said in part,

> It is really completely unrealistic to begin this discussion with the treaty of Riga. I admit that it is true . . . that the Soviet Government ultimately accepted the treaty of Riga, but nobody with a knowledge of the history of those parts is going to contend that Russia was content with that solution. . . . More than once we urged the Polish Government at the time not to extend their frontiers east beyond the Curzon Line and for two years after the treaty of Riga we withheld our recognition of that arrangement. In 1923, when the Conference of Ambassadors did eventually recognize those frontiers, that Conference made it plain on our initiative that the responsibility for the line [the Riga line of 1921] rested with the two governments concerned and not with us.[6]

5. Notable among these are Mr. Greenwood, Captain McEven, Lord Dunglass and Captain Graham.

6. From cables to the British Information Services in New York.

As to Eastern Galicia, for which the Allies proposed autonomy based on ethnographical reasons in favor of the Ukrainian majority, Mr. Eden said:

> The Eastern Galician area which is the only one, I think, in real dispute about the Curzon Line was an area of mixed population with Poles in the minority. The Poles sought to increase their own population in that area by bringing other Poles in with the result that that, in turn, led to friction.

On the other hand, Mr. Eden, more decisively than Mr. Churchill, upheld the plan of compensating Poland, in the west, at the expense to Germany of the former German provinces of East Prussia, the Baltic outlets and Upper Silesia. He concluded his remarks concerning the territorial issue as follows: "The new Poland when so constituted will be as strong or stronger than the Poland that existed in 1939. That depends of course on how the agreement is carried out."

The full importance of these statements by Mr. Eden has apparently escaped the attention which they deserve. There is a mistaken opinion, widely entertained, that Great Britain went to war to maintain the territorial integrity of Poland, including the guarantee of its eastern frontier. The question of the eastern frontier was not involved in Great Britain's declaration of war upon Germany. On September 3, 1939, Prime Minister Chamberlain made it clear to the House of Commons[7] that Britain entered the war because Hitler had refused every last measure of mediation and conciliation and was determined to resort to war with Poland in order to impose Germany's will upon that country. Although the question of Poland's western frontier—the Corridor and Danzig—were brought to the fore in Germany's statement of its case, the real issue for Great Britain was not the location of a boundary line but the refusal of the German Government to accept the pacific means of settlement which still remained open, until Hitler deliberately closed the door upon them. The question of the eastern frontier of Poland was certainly not in the mind of any British statesman at the time, because no such question had as yet arisen. Great Britain never at any time gave a guarantee for any specific line between Poland and Russia.

In the eyes of Polish nationalists, however, Great Britain's support of Poland was naturally interpreted as a support of the territorial integrity of the whole of Poland as it existed in 1939. This Polish point of view was expressed by Count Edward Raczynski, Polish Ambassador in Britain, who interpreted the treaty of 1939 as guaranteeing all of Poland's frontiers and

7. *Documents concerning German-Polish Relations and the Outbreak of Hostilities Between Great Britain and Germany on September 3, 1939,* Miscellaneous No. 9 (1939), London, H. M. Stationery Office, pp. 178-9.

not merely those on the west. The text of a secret protocol to this treaty has now been published and reads that Great Britain and Poland will support and assist each other against aggression by "a European power," but adds that by this phrase, *a European power,* is meant Germany. This treaty was made seven days before Germany attacked Poland. It is doubtful if any Englishman, within government circles or outside of them, thought through at that time the problem of the guarantee of Poland's eastern frontier; it did not become a problem until Russia invaded Poland in September of the same year.

The full story of British-Polish relations prior to the outbreak of the second World War in 1939 cannot yet be told, as the documents which deal with it are only beginning to appear. The main lines of policy are, however, clearly before us.

8. A New Polish Government

Looking Toward San Francisco

THE ESTABLISHMENT of the new Polish Provisional Government of National Unity, as provided by the Yalta Conference, became a question of political urgency after the calling of the Conference of the United Nations at San Francisco, April 25, 1945. If it were delayed, Poland would not be represented at the Conference. Some hope was expressed that Poland might receive an invitation, if a united representation could be agreed upon by the London Polish Government and the Warsaw administration, in time for the opening of the Conference. Prime Minister Arciszewski sent a note of protest against this, on March 12th, to the United States, Great Britain and China, and to all the other United Nations except the Soviet Union.[1]

According to an Associated Press dispatch of March 20, the United States and Great Britain launched a new effort in London to bring leaders of the Polish factions together with the hope of forming a representative

---

1. This note was published in *The Polish Review*, April 1, 1945. It reads in part as follows:

"Considering that the Polish nation took up arms in the defense of freedom, security and right on September 1, 1939, and was the first nation to make a stand against German aggression, and that from that time on, relentlessly and regardless of the sacrifice, it has been fighting at home and abroad, on land, on sea and in the air; considering also, that the Polish Nation has fought the longest in the defense of these ideals, and that it has sustained in relation to its potentialities heavier losses in human life and property than any other nation in the world; furthermore, considering that the war, begun in the defense of Poland, has created a spirit of unity among the free nations of the world which led to the promulgation and realization of the ideals of the United Nations; and finally, considering that at the San Francisco Conference the United Nations are to create a permanent world peace organization for the prevention of future aggression which is to be based on the respect of law and the sovereign equality of all peace-loving nations—the Polish Government as the sole legal and independent representative of the Polish state, emphatically insists on its indisputable right to take part in the world security conference and solemnly protests against its omission from invitation to the San Francisco Conference.

"The Polish Government wishes to state that not inviting to the San Francisco Conference Poland, whose constitutional President and Government are generally recognized by all the United Nations with the exception of only one of the powers and also by neutral states, is the first disquieting case of the application of the right to veto by a great power, which has been made even before the United Nations have approved or accepted proposals concerning an international security organization."

government so that Poland might send a delegation to the Conference. Fearing this might not be accomplished, Professor Oscar Lange, whose previous activities have been mentioned above at length, suggested a form of representation for San Francisco consisting of Edward Osubka-Morawski, Minister of Foreign Affairs of the Warsaw Polish Government, Tadeusz Romer, Minister of Foreign Affairs of the London Polish Government, and a third person to be designated jointly by these two.[2]

In the meantime one of the most important factors in the situation, following the Yalta Conference, was the decree of President Raczkiewicz, dated March 21, 1945, dissolving the Polish National Council in London, which since 1942 was the parliamentary basis of the Exile regime.[3] We have shown, in Chapter II, the exact political character of the Government coalition and the changes which had taken place in the shaping of this coalition. We have also seen that the Peasant Party and the Socialists were the leading groups in the National Council and the Government. With the resignation of Mikolajczyk, before the Yalta Conference, and with the appointment of Arciszewski, the leader of the right wing of Socialists, as the Premier, a breach in the whole set-up of the London regime had become inevitable. After the Yalta Conference, despite its legal recognition by Great Britain and the United States, the isolation of the London regime was complete; and its position was further undermined by internal discord between the Government and the National Council. Following the resignation of Mikolajczyk, the Peasant Party members of the Council and several Socialists, and even National Democrats and Christian Labor members, became an anti-Government majority in the Council.

Being uncertain about the support of its majority, the Government could not submit a protest against the Yalta decisions to the Council. In this desperate position, facing disintegration, the Government naturally tried to find a new basis upon which it could hold its position. In the decree of dissolution, President Raczkiewicz explained that the action was taken "in preparation for the organizing of a new Council more representative of the Poles inside Poland and in the liberated and other countries." The elements among which the Arciszewski regime hoped to find these adherents were Poles in the recently liberated western parts of Poland; in liberated countries like France where hundreds of thousands of Poles lived even before the war, employed as miners and industrial workers, and where other Poles were added as slave laborers under German occupation; and in other European countries. Even in Canada and the United States, Polish residents and their sympathizers were among the strongest supporters of Polish nationalist policies. The problem of a possible divided allegiance which this situa-

2. "Letters to The Times," *New York Times,* March 21, 1945.
3. *The Christian Science Monitor,* March 22, 1945.

tion tended to produce brought the Polish problem within the orbit of
domestic politics in other countries.

Tension on the Polish question continued. The International Commission provided for in the Yalta decision was "to consult in the first instance
in Moscow with members of the present Provisional Government and with
other Polish democratic leaders from within Poland and from abroad, with
a view to the reorganization of the present Government along the above
lines."

The Commission was installed early in February, but apparently its terms
of reference were not sufficiently clear, for it spent several weeks arguing
over two important issues. First, there was dispute as to the exact meaning
of the words in which the Yalta decision was couched. Marshal Stalin is
said to have insisted that the Polish Government was to be "reorganized"
merely by the addition of new members to the Warsaw Government, while
Prime Minister Churchill argued that a totally new government was intended. It has been asserted that, in letters so far unpublished,[4] President
Roosevelt criticized Mr. Churchill's interpretation, claiming that so extreme a position would leave the United States and Great Britain open to
charges of sabotaging the Yalta agreement. The second point of disagreement was not about who should be made members of the "new" or "reorganized" Polish Government, but over who should be allowed to go to Moscow to discuss with it the problem of forming the Government. The Warsaw Poles insisted on the right to veto any nominees advanced by Great
Britain and the United States.

After about seven weeks of uncertainty and hesitancy, the problem was
for the time being virtually taken out of the hands of the Commission by a
statement issued on March 31, 1945, by the TASS agency in Moscow. In
this statement the Soviet Government supported the request of the Provisional Warsaw Government that it participate in the San Francisco Conference. By such an act of diplomatic recognition the question of the nature
of the Polish Government would have been taken completely out of the
hands of the Commission and decided once and for all. It is by no means
clear that the Soviet Government meant to go this far; nor is it clear what
lay behind the gesture, which was quite in line with a form of diplomacy
formerly used at times by the Soviet Government when it was forcing a
point upon another Government. The language of the Soviet document
was almost that of a demand or an ultimatum, although later it was explained that this was not the case. The claim that Great Britain and the
United States should overlook the fact that there were no diplomatic relations between them and the Warsaw Government was based upon the argument that the Soviet Government in turn "had no diplomatic relations

4. *The Christian Science Monitor*, May 18, 1945.

with such countries as India, Haiti, Liberia or Paraguay," and yet went halfway to meet Britain and the United States by agreeing to the participation of these countries in the San Francisco Conference.

The incident was a puzzling one, giving the impression that there was something behind it not yet known to the public. In any case, the British and American Governments met the situation in the only way possible for them. They both refused to agree to the recognition of the Warsaw Government at San Francisco; they had earlier refused to allow the London Poles to attend. At the same time they set about clearing up the whole matter of Polish representation at that Conference.

In the middle of April it became known that both Governments had sent a note to Marshal Stalin expressing the hope that more rapid progress could be made in the work of the International Commission and seeking an explanation of the delay in bringing together representative Poles from inside and outside Poland to form a "Polish Provisional Government of National Unity" which all three Capitals could recognize. This note, however, apparently failed to produce action on the part of the Commission, which kept postponing agreement on the formation of a new Polish Government. President Roosevelt was apparently much concerned over the delay, and according to press reports, only a few days before his death sent a message to Marshal Stalin with reference to this matter.

The representation of Poland at the San Francisco Conference became more and more a matter of urgent concern not only to governments, but also to an alert public opinion. And then, ten days before the opening of the Conference, Mr. Mikolajczyk, the former Premier of the Polish Government-in-exile, after conferring with Foreign Secretary Anthony Eden, made an important statement in which he unequivocally endorsed the "Crimean decision in regard to the future of Poland, her sovereign independent position and the formation of a Provisional Government of National Unity" and accepted the Curzon Line as the eastern frontier of Poland. The former Premier also defined "close and lasting friendship with Russia as the keystone of future Polish policy."

Hopes for Poland's representation at San Francisco were revived by Mr. Molotoff's visit to Washington on his way to the Conference,[5] and by conversations between Secretary of State Stettinius, Foreign Secretary Eden and Mr. Molotoff at San Francisco, concerning the formation of a Provisional Polish Government. However, the visit to Washington proved unproductive and the conversations at San Francisco were abruptly broken

5. Mr. Molotoff's arrival coincided with the announcement of the conclusion on April 21, 1945, of a treaty between the Soviet Union and the Warsaw Polish Government; the treaty is to run for a term of twenty years, with provision for renewal in five year periods thereafter.

off after the sensational announcement of the arrest by Russia of sixteen members of the disbanded Polish Home Army.[6] Poland, the first to fling her armies against Nazi invasion, remained absent from San Francisco.

THE FORMATION OF A POLISH PROVISIONAL GOVERNMENT

The dangerous deadlock was finally broken through American intervention when President Truman sent Joseph Davies to London and Harry Hopkins to Moscow for discussions. As a result particularly of Mr. Hopkins' conversations with Marshal Stalin, President Truman was able to make an optimistic report on the situation on June 13. He pointed out that the discussions had shown conclusively that the "Russians were just as anxious to get along with us as we are to get along with them" and had yielded sufficiently to make agreement possible on the persons who were to meet in Moscow to discuss the formation of the new Provisional Government. The United States and Great Britain, on the other hand, had modified their original position concerning the sixteen arrested leaders in consenting to the initiation of these discussions prior to their release. According to the Crimean formula, Anglo-American recognition of the Provisional Government of National Unity would be forthcoming as soon as two conditions were met. It would have to be acceptable in composition to all three powers, and it would have to guarantee the holding of "free and unfettered" elections on the basis of universal suffrage and secret ballot—a point much pressed by President Roosevelt at Yalta and by Mr. Hopkins at Moscow.

Announcement of the long-delayed meeting of Polish leaders was made simultaneously in London, Washington and Moscow.[7] The terms of the communiqué solved the difficulties encountered in interpreting the Yalta agreement by evasion rather than by a direct interpretation. It spoke both

6. Marshal Stalin categorically denied London Government claims that Russia had invited the sixteen Poles for negotiations, and charged that they had been guilty of "diversionist" activities in the rear of the Red Army, such as blowing up bridges, killing Soviet soldiers, and so on. At the trial the men were also accused of participating in a plot to form an anti-Soviet bloc in Western Europe. Twelve of the accused, led by Major General Leopold Okulicki, pleaded guilty and three, partly guilty.

Throughout the public trial the major responsibility was laid at the door of the London Government and for that reason the sentences were fairly light, ranging from ten years to four months imprisonment. The heaviest punishment was meted out to General Okulicki, Polish Home Army Commander who had been sent to Poland in June, 1944, during German occupation, on the order of General Sosnkowski and against the wishes of Mr. Mikolajczyk.

While the trial was being held, the London Poles expressed satisfaction over the fact that a patriotic organization had continued to exist in Poland under the Russians. Though the Army had been disbanded in February, 1945, they admitted that it had been ordered to keep in contact with the London Government.

7. *New York Times,* June 13, 1945.

of the "reorganization of the Provisional Polish Government" and of the "formation of a Polish Provisional Government." The document seems to have been deliberately phrased so as to satisfy both Russian and Anglo-American interpretations and thereby make it possible to proceed to the really important business of the discussions themselves.

The International Commission, resuming its work, agreed on a list of Polish leaders to be invited to come to Moscow by June fifteenth, so that Polish problems could be solved by the Poles themselves. The first of the three groups was made up of representatives of the Polish Provisional Government and included President Boleslaw Bierut, Premier Edward Osubka-Morawski, Vice Premier Wladyslaw Gomolka, and Wladyslaw Kowalski. The group of democratic leaders from Poland included the eminent and non-partisan scholar, Dr. Henry Kolodzeiski, adviser to every premier of modern Poland; Zygmunt Zulawski, chairman of the National Council of the Socialist Party and Secretary General of the Polish Federation of Labor; and two professors from the University of Cracow, Stanislaw Kutrzeba, historian, and Adam Krzyzanowski, economist. Wincenty Witos, aged leader of the Peasant Party and twice Premier of Poland, could not attend because of illness.

The third group, of democratic leaders from abroad, was headed by former Premier Stanislaw Mikolajczyk. The two other delegates were Jan Stanczyk, former Minister of Social Welfare and Labor in the London Government, and a Socialist leader, and Anton Kolodziej, little-known head of the Polish Seamen's Union of Britain, which had early declared itself for the Warsaw Government. It is significant but not surprising that no members of the Government-in-exile were invited by the International Commission. No matter what their purely legal claims, the search for a workable solution of Polish problems had left them far behind.

Discussions among the Poles began hopefully in Moscow at the same time that the sixteen arrested Polish army members were being tried in the same city. On June 22, only five days after the initiation of the conversations, the Moscow radio announced the formation of a new Polish National Government. The Warsaw Government resigned and was replaced on June 28 by the Provisional Government of National Unity.

The composition of the Cabinet, Home National Council and Presidium of the new Government should allay Russian fears of a hostile neighbor, as the Warsaw Poles are assured of more than a comfortable working majority on all of them. The Cabinet consists at the moment of writing of twenty members, sixteen from the defunct Warsaw Government, three from the Peasant Party and one Socialist. The Premier, Mr. Osubka-Morawski, will be assisted by Vice Premier Gomolka, Secretary General of the Polish Workers' or Communist Party, and by the Second Vice Premier,

Mr. Mikolajczyk, who will also hold the important position of Minister of Agriculture. In addition to Mr. Mikolajczyk, Peasant Party representatives on the Cabinet are: Czeslaw Wicek, former chairman of the Teachers' Union of Poland and Underground educational leader, who is Minister of Education, and Wladyslaw Kiernik, Minister of Public Administration. Meczislaw Thugutt has declined an invitation to join the Cabinet as Minister of Post, Telephones and Telegraph. Jan Stanczyk, Socialist leader, will be Minister of Labor.

The Home National Council serves as the parliamentary body of the new Government. Those Poles who took part in the Moscow Conference but are not members of the Cabinet will join the other Councillors, who served throughout the life of the Warsaw Government.

The Provisional Presidium of the Home National Council is to exercise the vast powers formerly concentrated in the Presidency. The five members of the Presidium of the Warsaw Government will be joined by Wincenty Witos and by Professor Stanislaw Grabski, Social Democrat from abroad. Boleslaw Bierut will continue as chairman. The division of authority between the Cabinet and the somewhat unwieldy Presidium is not yet known. Evidently each is to exercise substantial powers.

No formal announcement of the elections which the Provisional Government is to hold has yet been made. According to newspaper reports, these elections can only be held in a year and will be governed by the electoral law of 1921, which provided for proportional representation and voting on party lists for each constituency. However, the new Government has taken the initial step of asking all Poles whose democratic leanings are unquestioned, to return to Poland. Anyone who was active in the Pilsudski-Beck regimes of 1926 to 1939, as well as members of the Government-in-exile and of its Foreign Office, will not be welcome in the new Poland. Prime Minister Churchill has declared that no Pole may be forced to return to his homeland against his will and, on February 27, 1945, he offered citizenship in the Commonwealth to members of the Polish Army in England, subject to Dominion approval. How many will accept this offer is not yet known.

The repatriation of refugee Poles is the most immediate problem facing the Warsaw Government, as quick reconstruction depends on sufficient manpower. The Russian-Polish agreement of July 7, 1945[8] removes a serious stumbling block in the path of their return. According to this agree-

8. *New York Times*, July 8, 1945. The agreement also provides that Russians, Ukrainians, White Russians, Ruthenians and Lithuanians anywhere in Poland may elect citizenship in the Soviet Union and move to Russia. All applications for change in citizenship are to be made by November 1, 1945, and all issues arising from the working out of this agreement for the exchange of populations will be dealt with by a mixed commission set up in Moscow.

ment, those Poles who became Soviet citizens through the Red Army's occupation of Eastern Poland in 1939 are now free to apply for Polish citizenship and to move west of the Polish-Russian border. These Poles were never
considered Russian citizens by Poles abroad, and their fate was bitterly re-
sented.

On July 5, 1945, Great Britain and the United States simultaneously announced their recognition of this Government, on the basis of its acceptance
of the Crimean decisions.[9]

Naturally the reaction of the Government-in-exile was one of extreme
hostility. It repudiated the Crimean decisions and all acts flowing from
them. In spite of the fact that Anglo-American recognition has been withdrawn, the President of the Government-in-exile, Wladyslaw Rackiewicz,
has implied that he intends to maintain his office, as under the Polish Constitution of 1935, the President can function as a single authority during an
emergency. With the organization of the Polish Provisional Government,
the Polish Army in England will continue to serve under the British Army's
Operational Command. The Polish Army in England has issued a statement of its loyalty to President Rackiewicz, referring to him as the "constitutional head of the Polish nation and of the Polish forces," and omitting
all references to the other organs of the government.

Meanwhile the international position of the Provisional Government of
National Unity is improving. Steps have been taken to ease Poland's re-
entry into international activities and co-operation. Though she was not
represented at San Francisco, Poland can nevertheless become an original
member of the new world organization because, according to the terms of
the Charter, such membership is also open to "states," not "governments,"
that signed the United Nations Declaration in January, 1942. Space has
been reserved for Poland's signature to the Charter in the alphabetical
list of signatories.

THE BERLIN CONFERENCE

As far as the problems of Poland are concerned, the Berlin Conference
built on the foundations laid at Yalta. Five months after that earlier meeting, the formation of a Provisional Government according to the Crimean
decisions was "noted with pleasure" by the heads of the three governments
assembled at Berlin.[10] President Truman, Generalissimo Stalin, and the
Prime Minister of Great Britain, Mr. Churchill, "together with Mr. Clem-
ent R. Atlee", also remarked on the establishment of diplomatic relations
with the new Government by the United States and Great Britain, accord-

9. See *New York Times*, July 6, 1945. Czechoslovakia, France, Sweden, Norway, Switzer-
land, and Canada have also already recognized the provisional Government.

10. Report on the Tripartite Conference of Berlin, Section IX, Poland. See Appendix VII.

ing to the conditions laid down at Yalta, and administered the coup de grâce to the Government-in-exile, which, they said, with the withdrawal of recognition, "no longer exists". Furthermore, as the Provisional Government is the recognized Government of Poland, the United States and Great Britain pledged themselves to protect its interests in property belonging to the Polish State located in their territory or under their control.[11]

That the fixing of Poland's boundaries is accompanied by numerous difficulties has been amply demonstrated in this study. At Yalta the troublesome Russo-Polish frontier was marked out with a fair degree of exactitude. The Polish-German boundary, on the contrary, was dealt with in general terms, with the Poles being promised "substantial accessions in the west and north." The form which these accessions are to take was worked out at Berlin, although, according to the Yalta terms, its final determination awaits the peace conference. According to Yalta, again, the opinion of Polish Government leaders was sought and a temporary line decided upon. According to the Report, Poland is to administer the following areas: former German territories east of a line running from the Baltic Sea immediately west of Swinemuende and thence along the Oder River to the confluence of the Western Neisse River and along the Western Neisse to the Czechoslovak frontier;[12] that part of East Prussia which is not placed under the administration of the Union of Soviet Socialist Republics; and the area of the former City of Danzig. With these additions to her territory, Poland will possess greatly increased industrial resources and will also find realization of an old dream, that of free and secure access to the Baltic Sea.

The Peace Conference will have the final decision on the extent of the territory taken from Germany, but there have been no indications at the time this book goes to press as to when it will be convened or what will be its nature. However, the fact that reference is made to it in the report of the "preliminary" negotiations at Potsdam would seem to imply that the Big Three expect it to examine and perhaps reconsider even such major issues as this. If it follows the notable example of the San Francisco Conference, it will not hesitate to take whatever action seems necessary in the interests of European peace. It is no part of this study to consider the conse-

11. After the Yalta decisions, the social welfare, education and finance departments of the Government-in-exile, which had been supported by Great Britain since 1941 as part of the common war effort, had been placed under joint British-Polish administration until they could be turned over without disturbance to the Polish Government in Warsaw.

12. Nothing is said in the Berlin Report concerning the great port of Stettin, which lies close to Swinemuende. According to newspaper reports, a sizeable migration of Poles into that city seems to be taking place.

13. Important to the success of these provisions is the decision, reported in Section XIII, to remove to Germany the German population of Poland.

quences of Russia's conquest of Koenigsberg and other ports of the Baltic, but the repercussions upon the future fortunes of Poland are too evident to need comment.

It will be evident from what has just been said that this study of Polish-Russian relations is not complete without a discussion of Poland's relations with Germany. The detailed analysis of that subject, however, would carry us far afield, for the end of the war is only the beginning of a new chapter of that history which, in 1939, seemed to reach a tragic close in the embers of Warsaw. The theme of this volume, however, properly ends at the Berlin, or Potsdam, Conference, where the deadlock among the Big Three was at last broken.

This is a hopeful sign for their co-operation, a co-operation which is essential for the healthy growth of the infant organization born at San Francisco. But Poland's fundamental problems still remain. As we have stated in the course of this study, they are only partly political. We must not forget that although the strength of a nation is tested by its relations with its neighbors, it rests in the last analysis upon its own healthy development in the fields of economic and social welfare and the guarantees of individual freedom.

Russia and Poland are linked to each other by geography. Therefore for Russia the hostility or friendship of the Polish Government have an immediate urgency which cannot be shared by the United States and Great Britain. A friendly Poland and a boundary closely approximating the Curzon Line mean a secure western flank for Russia. A hostile Poland awakens memories of the *cordon sanitaire,* of the Treaty of Riga, and adds to the potential menace of Germany. There is nothing new in the fact that all countries, no matter what their size or power, are basically interested in their security, as they interpret that difficult word. From the very nature of things, Russia has had and will continue to have a strong interest in the way Poland solves her problems. But this interest will be equally shared by Germany in years to come. In this difficult situation Poland's future will depend to a greater and greater degree upon the development of its own internal strength by measures of economic and social betterment for all people living within its new frontier.

This leads to a question the answer to which is more uncertain: that of the future development of the Polish Government. The elections which are to be held to transform the Provisional Government into a permanent one will furnish at least a partial key to the future of Poland. It is to be hoped that they result in a genuinely independent government, representative of many groups, healthily conscious of Polish history and tradition, and aware of the practical importance to Poland of good neighborly relations with Russia.

APPENDICES

AND

BIBLIOGRAPHY

APPENDIX I

NOTE OF THE U.S.S.R. DELIVERED TO POLISH AMBASSADOR IN MOSCOW
Concerning the Movement of Soviet Troops into Polish Territory—
September 17, 1939[1]

Mr. Ambassador,

The Polish-German War has revealed the internal insolvency of the Polish State. In the course of ten days of military occupation Poland has lost all her industrial districts and cultural centers. Warsaw as the capital of Poland, no longer exists. The Polish Government has disintegrated and shows no sign of life. This means that the Polish State and its government have virtually ceased to exist. Thereby the treaties concluded between the U.S.S.R. and Poland have ceased to operate. Left to herself and without leadership Poland has become convenient ground for any contingency and unexpected happenings which may create a menace to the U.S.S.R. Hence, having remained neutral until now, the Soviet Government can no longer maintain a neutral attitude to these facts. Nor can the Soviet Government remain indifferent to the fact that the kindred Ukrainians and Byelo-Russians living on the territory of Poland, abandoned to their fate, have been left defenseless.

In view of this situation the Soviet Government has instructed the high command of the Red Army to order troops to cross the frontier and to take under their protection the lives and property of the population of Western Ukraine and Western Byelo-Russia.

At the same time the Soviet Government intends to take all measures to deliver the Polish people from the disastrous war into which they have been plunged by their unwise leaders and to give them the opportunity to live a life of peace.

Accept, Mr. Ambassador, assurances of my highest consideration.

V. MOLOTOV
Peoples' Commissar of Foreign Affairs
of the U.S.S.R.

1. *Soviet Russia Today,* Oct. 1939.

APPENDIX II

DECLARATION OF THE POLISH GOVERNMENT
January 5, 1944[1]

In their victorious struggle against the German invader, Soviet forces are reported to have crossed the frontier of Poland.

This fact is another proof of the breaking-down of German resistance and it foreshadows the inevitable military defeat of Germany. It fills the Polish nation with hope that the hour of liberation is drawing near. Poland was the first nation to take up the German challenge and it has been fighting against the invaders for more than four years, at a cost of tremendous sacrifices and suffering, without producing a single Quisling and rejecting every form of compromise or collaboration with the aggressor.

The underground movement, among its many activities, concentrated upon attacking the Germans in their most sensitive spots, upon sabotage in every possible form and upon carrying out many death sentences on German officials whose conduct has been particularly outrageous.

Polish forces, twice reorganized outside their country, have been fighting ceaselessly in the air, at sea and on land, side by side with our Allies, and there is no front on which Polish blood has not mingled with the blood of other defenders of Poland.

There is no country in the world where Poles have not contributed to furthering the common cause. The Polish nation, therefore, is entitled to expect full justice and redress as soon as it is set free from enemy occupation.

The first condition of such justice is the earliest re-establishment of Polish sovereign administration in the liberated territories of the Polish Republic, and the protection of the lives and property of Polish citizens.

The Polish Government, as the only legal steward and spokesman of the Polish nation, recognized by Poles at home and abroad as well as by the Allied and free governments, is conscious of the contribution of Poland to the war and is responsible for the fate of the nation. It affirms its indestructible right to independence, confirmed by the principles of the Atlantic Charter common to all the United Nations and by binding international treaties.

The provisions of those treaties, based on the free agreement of the parties, not on the enforcement of the will of one side to the detriment of the other, cannot be reviewed by accomplished facts. The conduct of the Polish nation in the course of the present war has proved that it has never recognized and will not recognize solutions imposed by force.

1. Appendices II, III, IV, V quoted from *Polish Facts and Figures,* Polish Information Center, N. Y., March 25, 1944.

The Polish Government expects that the Soviet Union, sharing its view as to the importance of future friendly relations between the two countries, in the interests of peace and with the view of preventing German revenge, will not fail to respect the rights and interests of the Polish Republic and its citizens.

Acting in that belief, the Polish Government instructed the underground authorities in Poland on October 27, 1943, to continue and to intensify their resistance to the German invaders, to avoid all conflicts with Soviet armies, entering Poland in their battle against the Germans and to enter into cooperation with Soviet commanders in the event of resumption of Polish-Soviet relations.

If a Polish-Soviet agreement, such as the Polish Government has declared itself willing to conclude, had preceded the crossing of the frontier of Poland by Soviet forces, such an agreement would have enabled the Polish underground army to coordinate its action against the Germans with Soviet military authorities.

The Polish Government still considers such an arrangement highly desirable. At this crucial moment, the importance of which in relation to the outcome of the war in Europe is evident to everyone, the Polish Government issues the above declaration, confident in final victory and in the triumph of the just principles for which the United Nations stand.

This declaration has been handed to all the United Nations with which the Polish Government had diplomatic relations.

APPENDIX III

DECLARATION OF THE SOVIET GOVERNMENT
January 11, 1944

On January 5, a declaration of the exiled Polish Government on the question of Soviet-Polish relations was published in London. It contained a number of erroneous affirmations, including an erroneous affirmation concerning the Soviet-Polish frontier.

As is known, the Soviet Constitution established a Soviet-Polish frontier corresponding with the desires of the population of the Western Ukraine and Western White Russia, expressed in a plebiscite carried out on broad democratic principles in the year 1939. The territories of the Western Ukraine, populated in an overwhelming majority by Ukrainians, were incorporated in the Soviet Ukraine, while the territories of Western White Russia, populated in an overwhelming majority by White Russians, were incorporated in Soviet White Russia.

The injustice caused by the Riga Treaty in the year 1921, which was forced on the Soviet Union, with regard to Ukrainians inhabiting the Western Ukraine and White Russians inhabiting Western White Russia, was thus rectified. The entry of the Western Ukraine and Western White Russia into the Soviet Union not only did not interfere with the interests of Poland but, on the contrary, created a reliable basis, for a firm and permanent friendship between the Polish people and the neighboring Ukrainian, White Russian and Russian peoples.

The Soviet Government has repeatedly declared that it stands for the re-establishment of a strong and independent Poland and for friendship between the Soviet Union and Poland. The Soviet Government declares that it is striving toward the establishment of friendship between the U.S.S.R. and Poland on the basis of firm good-neighborly relations and mutual respect, and, should the Polish people so desire, on the basis of an alliance of mutual assistance against the Germans as the principal enemies of the Soviet Union and Poland. Poland's adherence to the Soviet-Czecho-slovak treaty of friendship, mutual assistance and post-war co-operation could assist in the realization of this task.

The successes of Soviet troops on the Soviet-German front speed day by day the liberation of the occupied territories of the Soviet Union from the German invaders. The selfless struggle of the Red Army and the fighting operations of our Allies that are unfolding bring the rout of the Hitlerite war machine nearer and bring liberation to Poland and other nations from the yoke of the German invaders.

In this war of liberation the Union of Polish Patriots in the U.S.S.R. and the Polish army corps created by it and operating on the front against the Germans hand in hand with the Red Army are already fulfilling their gallant tasks.

Now an opportunity for the restoration of Poland as a strong and independent State is opening. But Poland must be reborn, not by the occupation of Ukrainian and White Russian territories, but by the return of territories seized from Poland by the Germans. Only thus can confidence and friendship among the Polish, Ukrainian, White Russian and Russian peoples be established. The eastern borders of Poland can be fixed by agreement with the Soviet Union.

The Soviet Government does not consider the frontiers of the year 1939 to be unchangeable. The borders can be corrected in favor of Poland on such lines that districts in which the Polish population predominates be handed over to Poland. In such case the Soviet-Polish border could approximately follow the so-called Curzon Line, which was adopted in the year 1919 by the Supreme Council of Allied Powers and which provided for the incorporation of the Western Ukraine and Western White Russia into the Soviet Union.

Poland's western borders must be extended through the joining to Poland of age-old Polish lands taken away from Poland by Germany, without which it is impossible to unite the whole of the Polish people in its own state, which thus will acquire a necessary outlet to the Baltic Sea.

The just striving of the Polish people for complete unity in a strong and independent state must receive recognition and support. The émigré Polish Government, cut off from its people, proved incapable of establishing friendly relations with the Soviet Union. It has proved equally incapable of organizing an active struggle against the German invaders in Poland itself. Moreover, with its wrong policy, it frequently plays into the hands of the German invaders. At the same time, the interests of Poland and the Soviet Union lie in the establishment of firm and friendly relations between our two countries and in the unity of the Soviet and Polish peoples in the struggle against the common outside enemy, as the common cause of all the Allies requires.

APPENDIX IV

STATEMENT OF THE POLISH GOVERNMENT OF
January 15, 1944

The Polish Government has taken cognizance of the declaration of the Soviet Government contained in a TASS communiqué of the 11th of January, issued as a reply to the declaration of the Polish Government of January 5th.

The Soviet communiqué contains a number of statements to which complete answer is afforded by the ceaseless struggle against the Germans waged at the heaviest cost by the Polish Nation under the direction of the Polish Government. In their earnest anxiety to safeguard complete solidarity of the United Nations, especially at this decisive stage of their struggle against the common enemy, the Polish Government considers it preferable now to refrain from further public discussion.

While the Polish Government cannot recognize unilateral decisions or accomplished facts which have taken place or might take place on the territory of the Polish Republic, they have repeatedly expressed their sincere desire for the Polish-Soviet agreement on terms which would be just and acceptable to both sides.

To this end the Polish Government is approaching the British and the United States Governments with a view to securing through their intermediary the discussion by the Polish and Soviet Governments with participation of the British and American Governments of all outstanding questions, the settlement of which should lead to friendly and permanent co-operation between Poland and the Soviet Union.

The Polish Government believes this to be desirable in the interest of victory, of the United Nations and harmonious relations in postwar Europe.

APPENDIX V
SOVIET "TASS" STATEMENT
January 17, 1944

In reply to the declaration made by the Polish Government in London on January 15, TASS is authorized to state:

First, in the Polish declaration the question of the recognition of the Curzon Line as the Soviet-Polish frontier is entirely evaded and ignored. This can be interpreted only as a rejection of the Curzon Line.

Second, as regards the Polish Government's proposal for the opening of official negotiations between it and the Soviet Government, the Soviet Government is of the opinion that this proposal aims at misleading public opinion, for it is easy to understand that the Soviet Government is not in a position to enter into official negotiations with a government with which diplomatic relations have been severed.

Soviet circles wish that it should be borne in mind that diplomatic relations with the Polish Government were broken off through the fault of that Government because of its active participation in the hostile anti-Soviet slanderous campaigns of the German invaders in connection with the alleged murders in Katyn.

Third, in the opinion of Soviet circles, the above-mentioned circumstances once again demonstrate that the present Polish Government does not desire to establish good neighborly relations with the Soviet Union.

APPENDIX VI
THE YALTA CONFERENCE DECISION REGARDING POLAND
February 12, 1945[1]

POLAND

A new situation has been created in Poland as a result of her complete liberation by the Red Army. This calls for the establishment of a Polish Provisional Government which can be more broadly based than was possible before the recent liberation of western Poland. The Provisional Government which is now functioning in Poland should therefore be reorganized on a broader democratic basis with the inclusion of democratic leaders

1. *Dept. of State Bulletin*, Vol. 12, No. 295, Feb. 18, 1945.

from Poland itself and from Poles abroad. This new government should then be called the Polish Provisional Government of National Unity.

M. Molotoff, Mr. Harriman and Sir A. Clark Kerr are authorized as a commission to consult in the first instance in Moscow with members of the present Provisional Government and with other Polish democratic leaders from within Poland and from abroad, with a view to the reorganization of the present Government along the above lines. This Polish Provisional Government of National Unity shall be pledged to the holding of free and unfettered elections as soon as possible on the basis of universal suffrage and secret ballot. In these elections all democratic and anti-Nazi parties shall have the right to take part and to put forward candidates.

When a Polish Provisional Government of National Unity has been properly formed in conformity with the above, the Government of the U.S.S.R., which now maintains diplomatic relations with the present Provisional Government of Poland, and the Government of the United Kingdom and the Government of the United States of America will establish diplomatic relations with the new Polish Provisional Government of National Unity and will exchange Ambassadors by whose reports the respective Governments will be kept informed about the situation in Poland.

The three heads of Government consider that the eastern frontier of Poland should follow the Curzon Line, with digressions from it in some regions of five to eight kilometers in favor of Poland. They recognize that Poland must receive substantial accessions of territory in the north and west. They feel that the opinion of the new Polish Provisional Government of National Unity should be sought in due course on the extent of these accessions and that the final delimitation of the western frontier of Poland should thereafter await the peace conference.

APPENDIX VII

REPORT ON THE TRIPARTITE CONFERENCE OF BERLIN[1]

IX. *Poland*

The Conference considered questions relating to the Polish Provisional Government and the western boundary of Poland.

On the Polish Provisional Government of National Unity they defined their attitude in the following statement:

A—We have taken note with pleasure of the agreement reached among representative Poles from Poland and abroad which has made possible the formation, in accordance with the decisions reached at the Crimea Confer-

1. *New York Times*, August 3, 1945.

ence, of a Polish Provisional Government of National Unity recognized by the three Powers. The establishment by the British and United States Governments of diplomatic relations with the Polish Provisional Government has resulted in the withdrawal of their recognition from the former Polish Government in London, which no longer exists.

The British and United States Governments have taken measures to protect the interest of the Polish Provisional Government, as the recognized Government of the Polish State, in the property belonging to the Polish State located in their territories and under their control, whatever the form of this property may be. They have further taken measures to prevent alienation to third parties of such property. All proper facilities will be given to the Polish Provisional Government for the exercise of the ordinary legal remedies for the recovery of any property belonging to the Polish State which may have been wrongfully alienated.

The three Powers are anxious to assist the Polish Provisional Government in facilitating the return to Poland as soon as practicable of all Poles abroad who wish to go, including members of the Polish armed forces and the merchant marine. They expect that those Poles who return home shall be accorded personal and property rights on the same basis as all Polish citizens.

The three Powers note that the Polish Provisional Government, in accordance with the decisions of the Crimea Conference, has agreed to the holding of free and unfettered elections as soon as possible on the basis of universal suffrage and secret ballot in which all democratic and anti-Nazi parties shall have the right to take part and to put forward candidates, and that representatives of the Allied press shall enjoy full freedom to report to the world upon developments in Poland before and during the elections.

B—The following agreement was reached on the western frontier of Poland:

In conformity with the agreement on Poland reached at the Crimea Conference the three heads of Government have sought the opinion of the Polish Provisional Government of National Unity in regard to the accession of territory in the north and west which Poland should receive. The president of the National Council of Poland and members of the Polish Provisional Government of National Unity have been received at the Conference and have fully presented their views. The three heads of Government reaffirm their opinion that the final delimitation of the western frontier of Poland should await the peace settlement.

The three heads of Government agree that, pending the final determination of Poland's western frontier, the former German territories east of a line running from the Baltic Sea immediately west of Swinemuende, and thence along the Oder River to the confluence of the western Neisse River and along the western Neisse to the Czechoslovak frontier, including that portion of East Prussia not placed under the administration of the Union of Soviet Socialist Republics in accordance with the understanding reached at this Conference and including the area of the former free city of Danzig, shall be under the administration of the Polish State and for such purposes should not be considered as part of the Soviet zone of occupation in Germany.

BIBLIOGRAPHY

GENERAL

Buell, Raymond Leslie, *Poland: Key to Europe.* (New York: Knopf, 1939)

Cardwell, Ann Su, *Poland and Russia.* (New York: Sheed, 1944)

Chamberlin, William H., *The Ukraine: a Submerged Nation.* (New York: Macmillan, 1944)

Coates, W. P., *The U.S.S.R. and Poland.* (October, 1939)

Doroshenko, Dmytro, *History of the Ukraine.* (Edmonton, Canada: The Institute Press, 1939)

Fisher, Harold H., *America and the New Poland.* (New York: The Macmillan Company, 1928)

Grabski, Stanislaw, *The Polish-Soviet Frontier.* (London, 1943)

Halecki, Oscar, "Polish-Russian Relations, Past and Present," *The Review of Politics.* (July, 1942) Vol. V, No. 13, pp. 322-338.

Humeyko, S. S., *The Ukrainian National Movement.* (New York, 1939)

Joachim, Joesten, *What Russia Wants.* (New York: World Book Company, 1944)

Kellock, Harold, *The Polish Boundary.* (Editorial Research Reports: Washington, February 15, 1944) Vol. I, No. 7.

Lord, Robert H., *The Second Partition of Poland.* (Cambridge, U.S.A., 1915)

―――― *Some Problems of the Peace Conference.* (Cambridge, 1920), Chapter V: "Poland."

McKee, John, *Poland, Russia and Our Honor.* (Glasgow, 1940)

Malinowski, W. R., "Towards a Polish-Soviet Understanding" (Supplement, *New Europe,* November, 1943)

Miller, David Hunter, *My Diary at the Conference of Peace,* with Documents. (Privately Printed) Vols. I, X, XV, XVI, XVII, XVIII, Map in Vol. XVII.

Mizwa, Stephen P., *Great Men and Women of Poland.* (New York: The Macmillan Company, 1942)

Murray, M., *Poland's Progress 1919-1939.* (London, 1944)

Nicolson, Harold, *Curzon, the Last Phase, 1919-1925.* (Boston: Houghton-Mifflin Company, 1934)

Novak, Frank, *Medieval Slavdom and the Rise of Russia.* (New York: Holt, 1930)

Paprocki, S. J., *Minority Affairs in Poland.* (National Research Institute: Warsaw, 1935)

Schmitt, Bernadotte, E., *Poland,* a Symposium (Berkeley, 1945)

Smogorzewski, Casimir, "About the Curzon Line and Other Lines." *Free Europe* (London, January, 1944); also by same author: "More about the Curzon Line." *Free Europe* (February, 1944)

Stalin, Joseph, *Marxism and National and Colonial Problems.* (London: Lawrence, 1936)

Sworakowski, Witold, "An Error Regarding Eastern Galicia in Curzon's Note to the Soviet Government." Reprint from *Journal of Central European Affairs,* April, 1944.

Temperley, H. W. V., *A History of the Peace Conference of Paris.* (London, 1924) Vol. VI. Published under the auspices of the Institute of International Affairs (H. Frowde)

Voroles, H. P., *The Ukraine and Its People.* (London, 1939)

Weyers, Dr. J., *Poland and Russia.* (London, 1943)

Symposium on Polish-Soviet Relations: "We Will Join Hands with Russia." By Professor Oscar Lange, Senator James N. Tunnell, The Rev. Stanislav Orlemanski, Corliss Lamont, and Leo Krzycki. (Published by the National Council of American-Soviet Friendship, New York, 1944)

The Ukraine's Claim to Freedom: Symposium by Edwin Bjorkman, S. O. Pollock, M. Hrushevsky, O. Hoetzsch, and others (New York, 1915)

POLAND

The Constitution of Poland. Congressional Record, Washington, D. C., *Foreign Relations of the United States,* 1920, Vol. 3.

Constitution of the Republic of Poland. Stanislas Car and Michael Potulicki (Polish Commission of International Law Cooperation: Warsaw, 1935)

Constitution de la republique de Pologne, Loi du 17 Mars, 1921. Bathelemy and Henri Grappin.

Official Documents Concerning Polish-German and Polish-German Relations: The Polish White Book. The Republic of Poland, Ministry for Foreign Affairs. London: Hutchinson, 1940.

Other British and Foreign State Papers, 1919 (H. M. Stationery Office: London, 1942) Vol. 112, pp. 971-972.

Polish Facts and Figures. (New York: The Polish Information Center, March 25, 1944) No. 1-9.

Poland Fights. Polish Labor Group (sponsored by American Friends of Polish Democracy, New York) 1943-1944.

Periodicals

Soviet Russia Today. An official Soviet Periodical, (New York, 1943-1944)

The Economist. (London, 1943-1944)

The Nineteenth Century and After. Published by Constable & Co. (London, 1942 and June, 1943)

RUSSIAN LITERATURE

Formy nacionalnavo dvizhenia, Pod redakciyeyou A. Kastelyanskavo, St. Petersburg, 1909. (The Forms of National Movements, edited by A. Kastelyansky): *Ukrainians,* by Prof. M. Hrushevsky; *White Russians,* by A. Novina; *Poles,* by L. Krzivicky and M. Roemer.

J. Heifec, *Galicia; Politicheskoe, administrativnoye i sudebnoe ustroistvo* (Political, Administrative and Judicial Order) Petrograd, 1915.

Baron B. Nolde, *Otcherki russkavo gosudarstvennavo prava* (Outline of Russian Constitional Law), St. Petersburg, 1911.

Ukrainski Vopros (The Ukrainian Problem) A Symposium of articles, Moscow, 1917.

M. Laserson, *Nacionalnost i gosudarstvenni stroj* (The State Order and National Minorities) Petrograd, 1918.

V. Lenin, *Sotchinenia* (Works) Vol. XVII, XVIII, XXV. (State Publishing House, Moscow, 1928, 1929)

J. Stalin, *Marxism and National and Colonial Problems* (Russian Edition) Published by the Communist Party, Moscow, 1938.

V. Durdenevski, *Ravnopravie yazykov v S.S.S.R.* (Legal equality of Languages in the U.S.S.R.) Moscow, 1927.

I. Trainin, *Bratskoye Sodruzhestvo narodov S.S.S.R.* (The Fraternal Community of the Peoples of the U.S.S.R.) Moscow, 1938.

Documents and Sources

Politika Sovietskoi Vlasti po Nacionalnomu Voprosu za tri goda: 1917-1920. (The Policy of the Soviet State in the Nationalities Problem for the years 1917-1920) Official edition of the Commissariat of Nationalities, Moscow, 1920.

Bolshaya Sovietskaya Encyclopaedia. (The Large Soviet Encyclopaedia), Vol. 46, under "Polish-Soviet War 1926."

Sovietskaya Rossiya i Polsha, Officialnye Dokumenty (Soviet Russia and Poland, Official Documents), Peoples' Commissariat for Foreign Affairs, Moscow, 1921.

A. Manusevitch, *K diplomatitcheskoi istorii voprosa o vostotchnykh granitczakh posle-Versalskoi Polshi* (Concerning the diplomatic history of the question of the eastern borders of post-Versailles Poland) Published in the *Istoritcheski Journal*, Moscow, 1944, Vol. 4/128.

Periodicals

Slavyane (The Slavs), Monthly review of the All-Slavonic Committee, Moscow 1943 and 1944.

Voina i Rabotchi Klass (War and the Working Class), Bi-Weekly, Moscow, edition of the "Trud," 1943 and 1944.

Izvestia, Pravda, and other leading Soviet papers.

POLISH LITERATURE

Leon Vasilevski, *Ukraina i sprawa ukranska* (Ukraine and its cause) Cracow, 1911.

Jan Dabski, *Pokoj Ryski* (Ian Dombski, The Peace of Riga) Warsaw, 1931.

W. I. Jaworski, *Ankieta o konstitucji z 17 marca, 1921* (A study of the Constitution of March 17, 1921) Cracow, 1924.

Livre Rouge. Zbior dokumentow dyplomatycznych, odnoszacyh sie do stosunkow rosyjsko polskich 1918-1920 (A collection of documents concerning Russo-Polish diplomatic relations 1918-1920).

Periodicals

Nowe Widnokregi (New Horizons) bi-weekly, Moscow.

Wolna Polska (Free Poland) weekly, Moscow.

Nowy Swiat (The New World) daily, New York.

Gazeta Tygodniowa (Weekly Gazette) Schenectady, N. Y.

Gwiazda (Star) weekly, Philadelphia.

Czas (Time) weekly, Brooklyn, N. Y.

Czas (Time) weekly, Winnipeg, Canada.

UKRAINIAN LITERATURE

N. Grigoriv, *Ukrainska borotba za derzavu rokach 1917-1929* (The Fight for the Ukrainian State in the years 1917-1929) Scranton, 1934.

Na Rozdoroshyi (On the Threshold), A Symposium. New York-Detroit, 1944.

Periodicals

Gromadski Golos (The Voice of the Commonwealth) New York, bi-weekly, Organ of the democratic opinion of the Ukrainian immigrants in America.

Svoboda (Freedom) A "rightist" organ, Jersey City, N. J.

Ukrainski Golos (The Voice of the Ukraine) bi-weekly, Winnipeg, Canada.

WHITE RUSSIAN LITERATURE

Documents

Interpelyatzi bielaruskikh poslau u Polski Soim, 1922-1926, Minsk, 1927. (Interpellations of the White Russian members of the Polish Sejm for 1922-1926). Documents on attacks and depradations upon workers and peasants in western White Russia.

Periodicals

Bielarus (White Russia) A Soviet Review, Moscow, 1944.